Target 9
Get back on track

Pearson Edexcel GCSE (9–1)
History

Anglo-Saxon and Norman England, c1060–88

Georgina Blair

Pearson

Published by Pearson Education Limited, 80 Strand, London, WC2R 0RL.

www.pearsonschoolsandfecolleges.co.uk

Copies of official specifications for all Pearson qualifications may be found on the website: qualifications.pearson.com

Text and illustrations © Pearson Education Ltd 2018
Typeset and illustrated by Newgen KnowledgeWorks Pvt. Ltd. Chennai, India
Produced by Out of House Publishing Solutions

The right of Georgina Blair to be identified as author of this work has been asserted by her in accordance with the Copyright, Designs and Patents Act 1988.

First published 2018

British Library Cataloguing in Publication Data
A catalogue record for this book is available from the British Library

ISBN 978 1 292 24527 0

Copyright notice
All rights reserved. No part of this publication may be reproduced in any form or by any means (including photocopying or storing it in any medium by electronic means and whether or not transiently or incidentally to some other use of this publication) without the written permission of the copyright owner, except in accordance with the provisions of the Copyright, Designs and Patents Act 1988 or under the terms of a licence issued by the Copyright Licensing Agency, Barnard's Inn, 86 Fetter Lane, London EC4A 1EN (www.cla.co.uk). Applications for the copyright owner's written permission should be addressed to the publisher.

Note from the publisher
1. While the publishers have made every attempt to ensure that advice on the qualifications and its assessment is accurate, the official specification and associated guidance materials are the only authoritative source of information and should always be referred to for definitive guidance. Pearson examiners have not contributed to any sections in this resource relevant to examination papers for which they have responsibility.

2. Pearson has robust editorial processes, including answer and fact checks, to ensure the accuracy of the content in this publication, and every effort is made to ensure this publication is free of errors. We are, however, only human, and occasionally errors do occur. Pearson is not liable for any misunderstandings that arise as a result of errors in this publication, but it is our priority to ensure that the content is accurate. If you spot an error, please do contact us at resourcescorrections@pearson.com so we can make sure it is corrected.

Contents

1 Selecting key features
Get started	1
Norman government	3
1 How do I identify a key feature?	5
2 How do I select supporting detail?	6
3 How do I ensure I don't include too much supporting detail?	7
Sample response	8
Your turn!	9
Review your skills	10

2 Writing strong paragraphs
Get started	11
The Anglo-Saxon Church and Lanfranc's reforms	13
1 How do I focus my paragraphs on answering the question?	15
2 How do I structure a strong paragraph?	16
3 How do I link back to the question?	17
Sample response	18
Your turn!	19
Review your skills	20

3 Analysing causation
Get started	21
Edward the Confessor and the House of Godwin	23
1 How do I build a causal argument?	25
2 How do I develop a causal argument?	26
3 How do I link causal arguments to the question?	27
Sample response	28
Your turn!	29
Review your skills	30

4 Evaluating cause in context
Get started	31
Anglo-Saxon resistance to Norman rule	33
1 How do I identify the features of context that are relevant?	35
2 How do I show the influence of context?	36
3 How do I evaluate the importance of context?	37
Sample response	38
Your turn!	39
Review your skills	40

5 Evaluating significance
Get started	41
Changes to landholding	43
1 How do I assess significance?	45
2 How do I show that significance can change?	46
3 How do I decide what is most significant?	47
Sample response	48
Your turn!	49
Review your skills	50

6 Evaluating consequence
Get started	51
The Harrying of the North	53
1 How do I identify a consequence?	55
2 How do I show that something is a consequence?	56
3 How do I decide on the main consequence?	57
Sample response	58
Your turn!	59
Review your skills	60

7 Making judgements
Get started	61
The Battle of Hastings and its aftermath	63
1 How do I use my information to make a judgement?	65
2 How do I deal with conflicting evidence?	66
3 How do I ensure I make a convincing judgement?	67
Sample response	68
Your turn!	69
Review your skills	70

8 Writing effective conclusions
Get started	71
Norman government	73
1 What are the features of an effective conclusion?	75
2 How do I show why one element is more important than others?	76
3 How do I construct an effective conclusion?	77
Sample response	78
Your turn!	79
Review your skills	80

Answers   81

Get started

1 Selecting key features

This unit will help you to develop the skills to answer the features question effectively. The skills you will build are how to:

- identify key features
- select supporting detail for key features
- avoid writing too much for key features questions.

In the exam, you will be asked to tackle questions such as the one below. This unit will prepare you to write your own response to this type of question.

> **Exam-style question**
>
> Describe **two** features of the Marcher earldoms. (4 marks)
>
> Feature 1
> ....
> ....
>
> Feature 2
> ....
> ....

Remember that relevant key features are things that were characteristic or typical of Anglo-Saxon or Norman England – not a single event, such as a minor battle. This means key features are things that were common or happened often, or continued for long periods of time.

The three key questions in the **skills boosts** will help you to answer the features question effectively.

| 1 How do I identify a key feature? | 2 How do I select supporting detail? | 3 How do I ensure I don't include too much supporting detail? |

Unit 1 Selecting key features   1

Get started

Read the student's answer to the key features question below and the marker's comments. One mark is awarded for each relevant feature; one mark is awarded for supporting information.

Exam-style question

Describe **two** features of the Marcher earldoms. (4 marks)

Feature 1

Earldoms were areas of land made up from different shires. The word 'earl' comes from the Danish word 'jarl', meaning chieftain. The Marcher earldoms were created in Hereford, Chester and Shrewsbury to provide security along England's borders with Wales and were therefore given to men like William FitzOsbern, who were highly trusted by William I. The Marcher earldoms were smaller and more compact than traditional Anglo-Saxon earldoms.

- *This is background material and is irrelevant. You are writing about Marcher earldoms, not defining earls and earldoms.*
- *Well supported key feature: 2 marks.*
- *This is not necessary as you have got your 2 marks.*

1 Read the student's answer for Feature 2.

Exam-style question

Feature 2

Marcher earldoms came with more power than other earldoms because they were so important for England's defence. For example, Marcher earls did not have to apply to the king for permission to build castles. Castles were vital to England's defence too, and William I built them all over England as a means of controlling the Anglo-Saxons. Also, Marcher earls did not have to pay taxes.

- **a** Underline (A) the key feature.
- **b** Circle (A) the supporting information.
- **c** Cross out ~~cat~~ anything irrelevant.
- **d** Draw 🖉 a vertical line (|) at the point in the answer where the student has done enough to get both marks.

Unit 1 Selecting key features

Norman government

This unit uses the theme of changes to England's government to build your skills in selecting key features. If you need to review your knowledge of this theme, work through these pages.

1 Draw lines linking each of the terms below with a description.

term	description
A King	a Often lords of the manor
	b Paid the king a form of tax in return for land-holding and instead of doing military service
B Tenant-in-chief	c Performed 40 days' military service each year
	d Performed labour service in return for land
	e Provided peace, law and protection for the kingdom
C Under-tenant	f Ran baronial courts
	g Some were free, others were tied to the land
D Peasant	h Vassal to no one

2 Tick whether the statements below are true or false.

		true	false
a	Stigand was Bishop of Canterbury and Winchester	☐	☐
b	Stigand had little control over the Church in different parts of England	☐	☐
c	Simony was the practice of taking money in return for giving out Church jobs	☐	☐
d	Lanfranc did away with archdeacons	☐	☐
e	Lanfranc believed that the clergy should be tried in Church-only courts	☐	☐
f	Lanfranc believed priests should be married, family men and part of the community	☐	☐
g	Lanfranc practised pluralism	☐	☐
h	Lanfranc had cathedrals in isolated, rural places knocked down	☐	☐

Remember this?

3) Who was the bishop of Bayeux? ....

4) Which of the following terms are Anglo-Saxon, which are Norman and which are both? ✓

Term	Anglo-Saxon ✓	Norman ✓	Both ✓
Burh			
Earl			
Fief			
Fyrd			
Marcher earldom			
Sheriff			
Thegn			
Witan			

5) For each group below, circle Ⓐ the odd one out and write ✎ why it is the odd one out.

a) William Rufus | Robert of Mortain | Odo of Bayeux | Robert Curthose

....

b) Winchester | Chester | Hereford | Shrewsbury

....

c) Domesday Book | under-tenants | forest law | silver pennies

....

6) Circle Ⓐ your answers to the questions below. There might be more than one answer for each question.

a) Which of the following were terms for measuring land?
- A Wapentake
- B Forest
- C Geld
- D Hide

b) Which of the following did the Domesday Book survey?
- A Land held
- B Taxes paid
- C How many people were married
- D Whether more tax could be paid

c) Which of the following applied to the royal forest?
- A Restrictions on cutting wood
- B Carrying hunting weapons was banned
- C Hunting dogs were banned
- D Wild boar were protected

d) Which of the following were not allowed by the Norman Church?
- A The king appointing bishops
- B Simony
- C Bishops doing homage to the king
- D The king controlling Church communication with the pope in Rome

4   Unit 1 Selecting key features

Skills boost

1 How do I identify a key feature?

Key features are things that are typical, clearly recognisable characteristics of a person, place or era in history. This skills boost will help you to identify key features.

Read these two examples of key features of William I's reign.

> William I won the Battle of Hastings on 14 October 1066. This is a fact. It might be important, but it is not a key feature. William I was a successful military leader. This is also a fact. He was a successful military leader **for a long time**. It is a **key feature** of William I's reign that he was a successful military leader.

> During William's reign, Anglo-Saxon earls Edwin and Morcar rebelled in 1068. It is a fact. It is **one of many examples** of Anglo-Saxon opposition to William I in the early years of his reign. Anglo-Saxon opposition was a **key feature** of William's reign.

(1) Tick ✓ the statements below that you think are key features of William I's reign. For those that you select, also tick ✓ the reason why.

	Key feature? ✓	Why? (Long-term trend) ✓	Why? (One of many such examples) ✓
A Lanfranc was regent of England in 1075			
B William used regents to govern in his absence			
C The feudal system			
D The Marcher earldoms were important for England's defence			
E William took land to punish disloyalty			

(2) Read this website extract found by a student during their research and underline (A) any relevant key features of William I's reign.

Text 1

> William I established the feudal system in England, at the top of which were his tenants-in-chief. Odo and William FitzOsbern, both Normans, were two of the most important. Tenants-in-chief were very powerful, having their own knights and much land. Their role was to help William defend and govern England. He also appointed regents to govern England in his absence. Queen Matilda frequently took this role. Odo and FitzOsbern both acted as regents for him too. However, their poor government and land grabbing caused a rebellion when they were regents for him in 1067.

> Is the text you have underlined a key feature?
> - Is it something 'typical' of William I's reign (where there are lots of examples of the same thing)?
> - Is it a long-term trend of William I's reign?

Unit 1 Selecting key features

2 How do I select supporting detail?

For each key feature, you will get 1 mark for supporting detail. It is important to choose information that is relevant and to avoid including unnecessary description. This skills boost helps you to understand how to select supporting details.

Good supporting details will be:
- relevant to the question
- specific facts or examples
- one of many relevant examples.

1 a A student asked to identify a feature of William I's reign has decided to write about the Norman government. Choose three statements from the table below that provide good supporting detail on this subject. Tick ✓ the appropriate boxes to explain your choices.

	Relevant ✓	Specific ✓	One of many examples ✓
A William increased his revenue by raising taxes such as the geld, which were based on land held			
B William appointed regents, like archbishop Lanfranc, to govern England in his absence			
C Most of William's tenants-in-chief were Normans			
D William's preferred successor was William Rufus			
E Under William, sheriffs had much greater powers and were appointed by him			
F William created powerful Marcher earldoms on the Welsh borders to secure his rule there			

b Which of the statements would provide the strongest supporting detail? (Those with the most ticks!)

....

2 A student wrote the following answer for Feature 1 to a question asking for two features of William I's government.

> One key feature of William I's government was his use of sheriffs. They were expected to control their shires and were answerable to William only, making them very powerful. There was resentment against the sheriffs as they were often involved in land-grabs from Anglo-Saxons. Another feature was that William used royal councils, much like the Anglo-Saxon Witan, when he needed advice or support. In 1085, for example, he called a council because there were fears of a Viking invasion.

a Underline Ⓐ the supporting detail.

b Cross out ~~cat~~ any unnecessary description.

Unit 1 Selecting key features

Skills boost

3 How do I ensure I don't include too much supporting detail?

The key features question is worth 4 marks: 2 marks per feature. Writing more than you need will not gain you extra marks and will waste time that could be spent tackling the weightier questions. This skills boost will help you judge correctly how much to write for the key features question.

Use the following pieces of advice to write a concise answer.

- Avoid 'filler' material that is irrelevant, unnecessary or contributes nothing of value; this includes background material and descriptions.
- One piece of supporting detail is sufficient. Use it and move on.
- Don't explain the historical terms you use (such as earldoms, fiefs, homage, feudal system). It will be clear from the way they are used whether you understand them.

A student has written an answer to the following exam-style question:

Exam-style question

Describe **two** features of knights in Norman England. (4 marks)

Feature 1

One feature of Norman knights was that they owed the king 40 days of knight service a year, making them an important and cheap way of providing defence for the kingdom because it was their lords who had to pay the bill. The Anglo-Saxon word for knight was 'cniht'. The word cniht/knight means 'household retainer', which means someone who follows an important person.

Feature 2

Knights had an important role in controlling England. They played a key part in law and order as they were often lords of the manor and settled disputes in their manorial courts. Tenants-in-chief also held their own courts. Norman knights were elite cavalry troops, vital to William's army. They were able to charge their opponents' ranks with devastating effect, causing them to scatter. Because they were on horseback, they had kite-shaped shields and their chainmail was split so that their legs were protected.

1. a Underline (A) any examples of irrelevant 'filler' material.
   b If the student provided two pieces of supporting detail for either key feature, cross out the second, unnecessary one.
   c Circle (A) any definitions of historical vocabulary.

> **Remember:** 'Filler' material is unnecessary background information or descriptions that do not directly address the focus of the question.

Unit 1 Selecting key features 7

Sample response

Selecting features and avoiding putting too much detail in your answers is important for any exam question. Once you have made and supported a point, move on. Writing down everything you know is not a skill. The skill is selecting and deploying relevant evidence.

Exam-style question

Describe **two** features of Marcher earldoms. (4 marks)

Feature 1

Marcher earldoms gave earls the rights that usually only the king had. They could build churches, establish markets and create boroughs so that the earldoms would develop faster and people would be attracted to live there. 'Borough' was another term like 'burh', both meaning town.

Feature 2

Marcher earldoms were smaller and more compact than traditional earldoms. This was to make them easier to defend, as English borderlands were frequently attacked by the Welsh. Anglo-Saxon earldoms were much larger. William replaced Anglo-Saxon earls with Normans. Sheriffs in Marcher earldoms worked for the earls, making the earls more powerful. In the rest of England they were answerable only to the king.

(1) Read the student's response above, then list 🖉 the strengths and weaknesses in the table, using the suggestions below to help you.

Do ...	Don't ...
• give key features rather than an event or one-off occurrence	• add any filler such as background or description
• make sure your key features are relevant	• provide more than one piece of specific supporting detail per feature
• provide specific supporting detail.	• include anything not relevant to the question or key feature.

	Strengths	Weaknesses
Feature 1		
Feature 2		

Unit 1 Selecting key features

Your turn!

1 Write ✏ an answer to the exam-style question below.

Exam-style question

Describe **two** features of the Anglo-Saxon Church. (4 marks)

Feature 1

....
....
....
....
....

Feature 2

....
....
....
....
....
....

2 Once you have written your answer, identify ✏ your answer's strengths and weaknesses using the suggestions on page 8.

	Strengths	Weaknesses
Feature 1		
Feature 2		

Unit 1 Selecting key features   9

Review your skills

Check up

Review your response to the exam-style question on page 9. Tick ✓ the column to show how well you think you have done each of the following.

	Had a go ✓	Nearly there ✓	Got it! ✓
identified relevant key features	☐	☐	☐
avoided 'filler' material (description, background, definitions)	☐	☐	☐
selected good supporting detail	☐	☐	☐
written no more than was needed	☐	☐	☐

Look over all of your work in this unit. Note down ✎ three things you have learned that you will apply when answering key features questions.

① ....
② ....
③ ....

Need more practice?

On separate paper, plan and write ✎ your response to the exam-style question below.

Exam-style question

Describe **two** features of motte and bailey castles. (4 marks)

Feature 1
....
....

Feature 2
....
....

How confident do you feel about each of these **skills**? Colour in ✎ the bars.

① How do I identify a key feature? ☐☐☐☐
② How do I select supporting detail? ☐☐☐☐
③ How do I ensure I don't include too much supporting detail? ☐☐☐☐

Unit 1 Selecting key features

Get started

② Writing strong paragraphs

This unit will help you to develop the skills to write strong paragraphs. The skills you will build are to:

- recognise what makes a strong paragraph
- structure strong paragraphs
- link paragraphs back to the question.

Strong paragraphs are focused and analytical. They have no 'filler' material. You should not write everything you know, but target what you include to focus directly on answering the question. This unit will prepare you to write your own response to questions like the one below, using strong paragraphs.

'Filler' is material that is not relevant to the focus of the question, such as background and unnecessary explanations. Descriptions or narrative with no clear link to the question focus are also unnecessary.

> **Exam-style question**
>
> Explain why Lanfranc reformed the Church in England.
>
> You may use the following in your answer:
>
> - Normanisation
> - simony.
>
> You **must** also use information of your own. (12 marks)

The three key questions in the **skills boosts** will help you to write strong paragraphs.

① How do I focus my paragraphs on answering the question?

② How do I structure a strong paragraph?

③ How do I link back to the question?

Unit 2 Writing strong paragraphs 11

Get started

Read the following paragraph from a student's response to the exam-style question on page 11.

> Lanfranc, who was known to be a reformer, replaced the Anglo-Saxon Archbishop of Canterbury, Stigand, in 1070. Lanfranc was very close to William. He became so powerful that he was able to crown William's favourite son king in 1087 without consulting anyone. Many of Lanfranc's reforms, which are known as Normanisation, greatly strengthened William I's position. For example, under Lanfranc, William I controlled all communication with the pope in Rome. The pope is the leader of the Roman Catholic Church. Lanfranc's reforms made the Church much more disciplined, with greater control over parish priests, who were made to follow Norman procedures and customs. The Church was also very important in making sure the people – especially the Anglo-Saxons – heard favourable things about the king. Priests taught that God was on the Normans' side at Hastings, for example. Lanfranc was very much William's man. He agreed that William must be in charge of communication between the pope and the English Church. This shows that Lanfranc's reforms were helpful to William I, strengthening his position.

1 a Cross out ~~cat~~ any 'filler' material in the answer.

b Look at the student's planning notes for the next paragraph about Lanfranc's reforms to the Church in England. Place a cross (X) alongside any points that are irrelevant to the question.

> A Lanfranc = Italian monk, teacher, lawyer; ran William's St Stephen's monastery in Normandy.
>
> B Lanfranc wanted Church separate from rest of society; priests to live spiritual, religious life – not like Anglo-Saxon priests (often married, had children, and lived as part of local communities).
>
> C Big reform movement in 11th-century Catholic Church. Popes wanted the clergy separate from secular government – kings often opposed this, wanted clergy to obey only them → tensions with the popes.
>
> D In 1076 Church Council agreed separate Church-only bishops' courts for clergy.
>
> E Lanfranc's reforms wanted Church separate from society, more spiritual, religious; reforms included ending marriage for clergy.
>
> F Lanfranc also wanted to end corruption – stopped pluralism and simony.
>
> G Simony = taking money in return for giving someone position in Church.
>
> H These reforms show that Lanfranc wanted a more religious, spiritual, disciplined Church.

Remember: Your second paragraph should have:
- an opening sentence that makes the point of the paragraph clear
- a final sentence that links the paragraph back to the question.

The Anglo-Saxon Church and Lanfranc's reforms

This unit uses the theme of the Anglo-Saxon Church and Lanfranc's reforms to build your skills in writing strong paragraphs. If you need to review your knowledge of this theme, work through these pages.

1 Draw lines linking each member of the clergy to its description.

clergy

- A Archbishop
- B Archdeacon
- C Bishop
- D Monks
- E Pope
- F Priests

description

- a Controlled a large group of parishes
- b Head of the Catholic Church in Rome
- c In charge of a parish
- d Lived together in monasteries
- e Oversaw discipline in the Church at local level
- f There were two in England: one in Canterbury and one in York

2 Circle your answers to the questions below. There might be more than one answer to each question.

a Which of the following roles did clergy often undertake?
- A Advised the king on developing laws and on legal matters
- B Acted as the king's representative
- C Wrote and issued writs
- D Enforced the king's will in manor courts

b Which of the following statements apply to Archbishop Stigand?
- A He was accused of simony
- B He was a close ally of Bishop Odo
- C He was Archbishop of Canterbury
- D He was Bishop of Winchester

c Which of the following statements apply to Archbishop Lanfranc?
- A He wanted clergy to be tried in special Church-only bishops' courts
- B He was an Italian monk
- C He crowned William Rufus in 1087
- D He was a close ally of Archbishop Stigand

3 Tick the main reason for the Normanisation of the Church.
- A To make Roman Catholicism the main religion in England
- B To strengthen Norman rule in England
- C To change church architecture in England

Unit 2 Writing strong paragraphs 13

Remember this?

4 Draw lines linking the beginning of each sentence with the correct ending.

beginning

A The Normanised Church taught that

B Lanfranc's reforms made sure that

C William's control of Church councils meant that

D Making them part of the feudal system ensured that

ending

a disloyal bishops could forfeit their lands.

b God favoured the Normans.

c the king's approval was needed for key decisions.

d parish priests came under much stricter control.

5 For each group below, circle (A) the odd one out and write why it is the odd one out.

a | archdeacons | abbots | archbishops | bishops |

....

b | York | Chichester | Lincoln | Durham |

....

c | regent | representative | adviser | sheriff |

....

6 Tick ✓ to show whether the statements below are true or false.

		true	false
A	Trials by ordeal came under the Church's control.	☐	☐
B	Under Lanfranc, the number of archdeacons increased.	☐	☐
C	Lanfranc introduced pluralism to save the Church money.	☐	☐
D	A Church council of 1067 passed Lanfranc's reform that court cases involving the clergy should be heard in special Church courts.	☐	☐
E	Lanfranc allowed already married priests to remain married.	☐	☐
F	Lanfranc was keen for the Church to remain as Anglo-Saxon as possible, to help the English accept Norman rule.	☐	☐
G	Under Lanfranc, the Archbishops of Canterbury and York were given equal status.	☐	☐
H	Building new cathedrals in more isolated areas helped the Normans to strengthen their hold on rural communities.	☐	☐

Skills boost

1 How do I focus my paragraphs on answering the question?

Students often write down everything they know in an answer for fear of missing something out. Strong paragraphs, however, are focused and analytical. This skills boost will help you to identify the key features of a strong paragraph.

Here are a student's notes for an answer to the exam-style question on page 11 on why Lanfranc reformed the Church in England.

A Normanisation of Church in England = helped to strengthen William and Norman rule.

B New churches built – Norman architecture – strong visual reminder to Anglo-Saxons of Norman rule.

C Norman architecture = high ceilings, ornately carved pillars, much deeper foundations, bigger buildings, e.g. Winchester Cathedral was longest in Europe.

D Cathedrals were moved from isolated, rural places → strategically important market towns so bishops were safer, stronger and had more control over their area.

E Cathedrals moved from Selsey → Chichester; and from Thetford → Norwich.

F Architectural changes accompanied by purge of the Church → only one Anglo-Saxon bishop left: Wulfstan in Worcester.

G Purge = getting rid of people you don't want, especially if they don't fit in.

H Wulfstan loyal to William; helped to put down the rebellion in 1075.

(1) Tick ✓ only the information above that is **necessary** to write a paragraph on why Lanfranc reformed the Church in England.

It is not necessary to explain historical words or terms in an essay unless they are in the title. Your understanding will be clear from how you use them. Read the paragraph below.

> In Norman England, the Church was a major landholder. It got its land from the king, like everyone else in William's new social hierarchy, with him firmly at the top. Bishops, like earls, were immediately under the king and got their land directly from him so had to provide him with knights for 40 days each year at their own expense. They were also required to publicly demonstrate their allegiance to William in a special ceremony in return for their fiefs. This made the Church subordinate to the king and useful for controlling England. Lanfranc especially was very loyal to William, even though the pope expected clergy to obey him first rather than non-ecclesiastical or non-religious leaders.

(2) Cross out the explanation/description in the paragraph above and write in the letter of the term from the list below that could be used instead.

A the feudal system   B pay homage   C knight service   D secular   E tenants-in-chief

Unit 2 Writing strong paragraphs   15

Skills boost

2 How do I structure a strong paragraph?

When starting a paragraph, don't 'set the scene' with extra background information that is irrelevant to the question. Begin with a point about the question that the paragraph is answering. The main body should be focused and concise, with no 'filler'. End with a link back to the question. This skills boost will help you to structure a strong paragraph.

A good opening sentence provides a clear link to the question by making a point about it.

(1) Tick ✓ which of the following would make the best start to a paragraph about why Lanfranc reformed the Church in England.

- **A** Lanfranc believed in a disciplined, spiritual Church and did not like what he found in England.
- **B** Lanfranc knew that a strong Norman Church in England would help to establish Norman control.
- **C** A strong and loyal government throughout England was important to William's takeover.

Here are some statements that a student included in a paragraph on Lanfranc bringing the Church in England into line:

- **a** Stigand, the old Archbishop of Canterbury, had been a close ally of Earl Godwin, whereas Lanfranc was a close ally of William I.
- **b** In Lanfranc's eyes, the English Church was corrupt and not very spiritual.
- **c** Lanfranc believed in a strict hierarchy, with the pope at the top, then cardinals, then archbishops, then bishops, then archdeacons and priests, etc.
- **d** There was also a wider reform movement in the Catholic Church across Europe at the time.
- **e** The English Church had different practices all over the country, which was unacceptable to Lanfranc, so he unified it under Norman guidelines and procedures.
- **f** This led to the important reform of more archdeacons.
- **g** Archdeacons enforced Church discipline, making it easier to control all of the priests in a diocese.

The student started their essay with statement **C**, then used statements **a–g** in their paragraph.

(2) Why is statement C not a good way to start the paragraph?

....
....
....

(3) Use the table below to evaluate the statements the student has chosen. Tick ✓ your choices.

Which statements ...	a ✓	b ✓	c ✓	d ✓	e ✓	f ✓	g ✓
have **unnecessary** description?							
are **not** focused on the question?							

(4) Which **four** statements would you use for the paragraph? Choose an introductory sentence from **(1)**, followed by **four** from **a–g**. ....

16   Unit 2 Writing strong paragraphs

Skills boost

3 How do I link back to the question?

To link your answer back to the question, you need to refer to the key points in it. Include some of the question's key words and phrases in each paragraph opening. End each paragraph with a clear judgement that is justified by referring back to the key words from the question. This skills boost will help you to link your paragraphs back to the question.

Here is a student's plan for the main body of an essay to answer the exam-style question on page 11.

> Paragraph 1:
> Important reform = rebuilding Church buildings along Norman lines = important as clear, visual reminder of Norman victory at Hastings (God's approval), plus Normanisation of the Church and England. Also rebuilt remote, isolated cathedrals (give example) in strategically important market towns (give example). Aim = to make bishops more secure plus better control (links to discipline, also key reform) over their areas → strengthening William's grip – another important reason for Church reform.
>
> Paragraph 2:
> Improve Church discipline = reform aim. Unify the English Church under Norman guidelines and standards; strict hierarchy, but under William – not the pope. Also, William = head of feudal system; bishops held land as vassals. Reforms for discipline = (i) unify Church; (ii) more archdeacons to enforce Church discipline, e.g. preside over Church courts; (iii) Church courts = reform to control parish priests.

The student then wrote the following paragraph based on the plan for paragraph 1:

> One reason for Lanfranc's reforms was to strengthen Norman control over England. One reform was to rebuild Church buildings. This was important for two reasons. Firstly, they would be made to look Norman, using Norman architectural features such as high, vaulted ceilings. They would be a visual reminder to the Anglo-Saxons of God favouring William at Hastings. Secondly, and more importantly, cathedrals in isolated locations (like Thetford) were demolished and rebuilt in strategically important market towns (like Norwich). This made Norman bishops more secure and enabled them to better control their clergy and their flocks. Thus this important reform was aimed at strengthening William's grip on England and the Anglo-Saxons.

(1) In the student's paragraph above:
   a. underline (A) where the student has made the point of the paragraph clear
   b. double underline (A) the explanation of the point of the paragraph
   c. circle (A) any evidence supporting the explanation
   d. cross out any 'filler' material or irrelevancies
   e. highlight clear links to the question focus, demonstrated by the use of key words from the question.

   Look at the plan: was there any 'filler'? Did the student make the mistake of including it?

(2) Identify the focus of the second paragraph on a separate piece of paper.

(3) Look at the plan for paragraph 2 and highlight those parts that are necessary to write a strong paragraph.

Unit 2 Writing strong paragraphs 17

Sample response

Strong, focused, analytical paragraphs with clear links back to the question are an important part of any written examination.

Read the following extracts from an answer to the exam-style question on page 11.

Paragraph 1

Lanfranc had religious aims when he reformed the English Church. As a religious, spiritual man, who was an Italian monk before he joined William to run St Stephen's monastery in Normandy, he was appalled at some of the practices he found in England. Lanfranc wanted reforms to separate clergy from everyday concerns such as making money, gaining power, marriage and children. This led to reforms that stopped clergy marrying and required them to be celibate, as well as ending the practices of pluralism and simony. These reforms were enforced by another: Church courts for clergy. Lanfranc also increased the number of archdeacons to do this. Archdeacons were members of the clergy below bishops. Their role was to enforce discipline, making it easier for the Church to get control over all parish priests. All of these reforms that Lanfranc brought in made it clear that the clergy were separate from the rest of society. This was not easy as the Church played an important part in government. Clergy were literate and were employed to write and issue the king's writs. Furthermore, bishops often helped to develop the law and advised the king on legal matters.

Paragraph 2

Lanfranc's reforms were also aimed at the Normanisation of the English Church. Normanisation meant that the Church was used to strengthen Norman control over England. The new Normanised Church was clearly seen in the Norman architecture of new church buildings, like Durham Cathedral. Winchester Cathedral was the longest in Europe. It wasn't only the design of buildings that was new. Cathedrals in isolated, rural areas, like Thetford, were relocated to strategically important market towns, like Norwich. This gave bishops more control over their areas as well as making them more secure. Lanfranc's reforms therefore aimed to support William I in strengthening his grip on England.

1 Write '1' and/or '2' in the table to identify the strengths and weaknesses of paragraphs 1 and 2.

Strengths		Weaknesses	
Paragraph opens with a clear point about why Lanfranc reformed the Church in England.		Paragraph contains unnecessary or irrelevant information (filler).	
Paragraph ends with a clear link back to the question.		Paragraph wanders off the question focus.	
A reason for Lanfranc's reforms is clearly explained with relevant evidence.		Paragraph contains unnecessary explanation of historical terms.	

2 Overall, how well do you think the student answers the question? Draw an arrow below to show your choice. Give the student one piece of advice to help them improve their answer.

1/6	2/6	3/6	4/6	5/6	6/6
No focus. Question not answered.	Poor. Largely without focus.	More unfocused than focused.	More focused than not.	Good answer. Well focused.	Excellent. Focused throughout.

Unit 2 Writing strong paragraphs

Your turn!

1. Rewrite ✎ the two paragraphs from the sample answer so that they give a more focused answer, with clear links back to the question. The sample answer is 298 words; try to write your answer in fewer than 200 words. Use the following prompts to help you.

Checklist	✓
Does your opening statement say what cause / consequence / change / feature the paragraph is addressing?	
Is your answer focused? Is it free from 'filler' material?	
Does your answer provide support for your explanation of the cause / consequence / change / feature you are writing about?	
Does your last statement link back to the question by stating: - how important the cause / consequence / change / feature is? - whether the cause / consequence / change / feature is more or less important than the stated cause / consequence / change / feature?	
Is the question wording in your answer?	

Exam-style question

Explain why Lanfranc reformed the Church in England.

You may use the following in your answer:
- Normanisation
- simony

You **must** also use information of your own. (12 marks)

Unit 2 Writing strong paragraphs

Review your skills

Check up

Review your response to the exam-style question on page 19. Tick ✓ the column to show how well you think you have done each of the following.

	Had a go ✓	Nearly there ✓	Got it! ✓
opened each paragraph with a clear point about the question	☐	☐	☐
ended each paragraph with a clear link back to the question, avoiding any 'filler'	☐	☐	☐
used historical terms without explaining them or describing what they mean	☐	☐	☐

Look over all of your work in this unit. Note down three things you have learned that you will apply when writing strong paragraphs.

1. ....
2. ....
3. ....

Need more practice?

On separate paper, plan and write your response to the exam-style question below.

Exam-style question

Explain why William I introduced the forest laws.

You may use the following in your answer:

- Royal demesne
- hunting

You **must** also use information of your own.

(12 marks)

How confident do you feel about each of these **skills**? Colour in the bars.

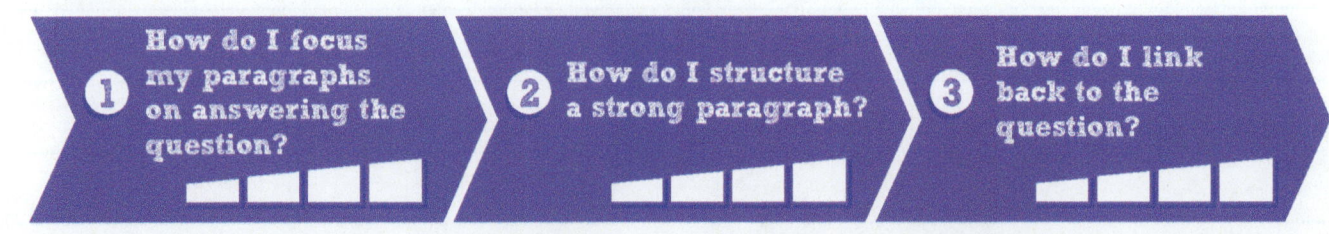

1. How do I focus my paragraphs on answering the question?
2. How do I structure a strong paragraph?
3. How do I link back to the question?

Unit 2 Writing strong paragraphs

Get started

③ Analysing causation

This unit will help you to develop the skills to analyse causation effectively. The skills you will build are how to:

- build causal arguments
- develop causal arguments
- link causal arguments to the question.

In the exam, you will be asked to tackle questions such as the one below. This unit will prepare you to write your own response to this type of question.

> **Exam-style question**
>
> Explain why the House of Godwin was a problem for Edward the Confessor.
>
> You may use the following in your answer:
>
> - Tostig
> - Wessex
>
> You **must** also use information of your own. (12 marks)

The three key questions in the **skills boosts** will help you understand how to analyse causation effectively.

① How do I build a causal argument?

② How do I develop a causal argument?

③ How do I link causal arguments to the question?

Unit 3 Analysing causation 21

Get started

Below are two students' plans for the following exam-style question:

> **Exam-style question**
>
> Explain why the House of Godwin was a problem for Edward the Confessor.
>
> You may use the following in your answer:
>
> - Tostig
> - Wessex
>
> You **must** also include information of your own. (12 marks)

Plan A

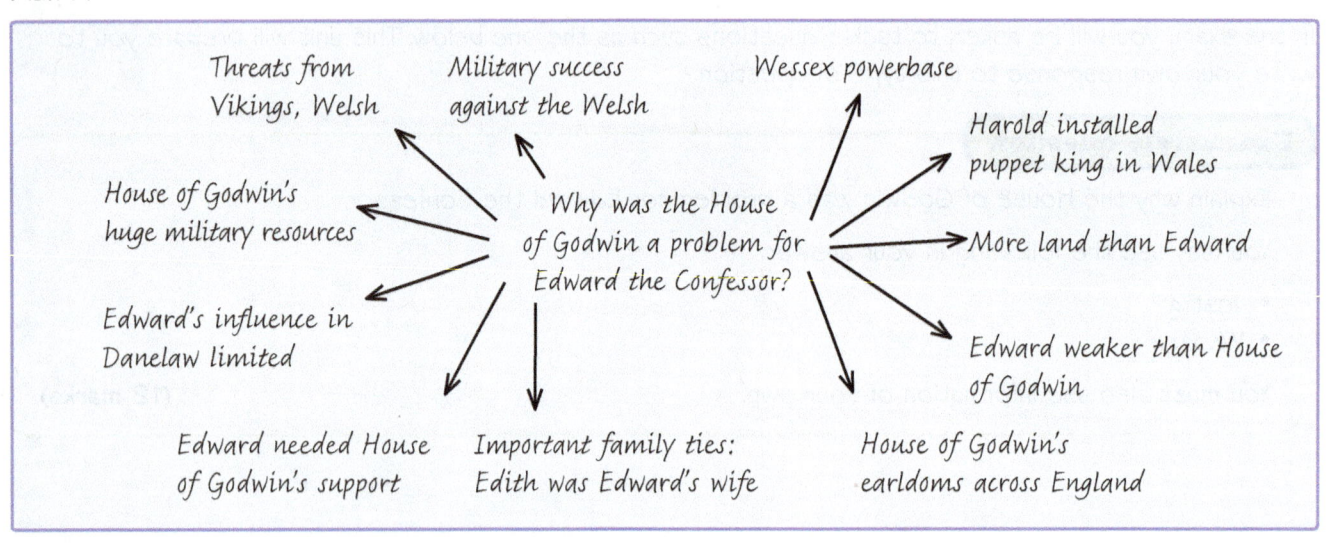

- Threats from Vikings, Welsh
- Military success against the Welsh
- Wessex powerbase
- Harold installed puppet king in Wales
- House of Godwin's huge military resources
- More land than Edward
- Edward's influence in Danelaw limited
- Edward weaker than House of Godwin
- Edward needed House of Godwin's support
- Important family ties: Edith was Edward's wife
- House of Godwin's earldoms across England

Central question: Why was the House of Godwin a problem for Edward the Confessor?

Plan B

Edward's weakness in England + Threats from Vikings and Welsh → House of Godwin's wealth and strength = House of Godwin a problem for Edward

↑ House of Godwin's military success

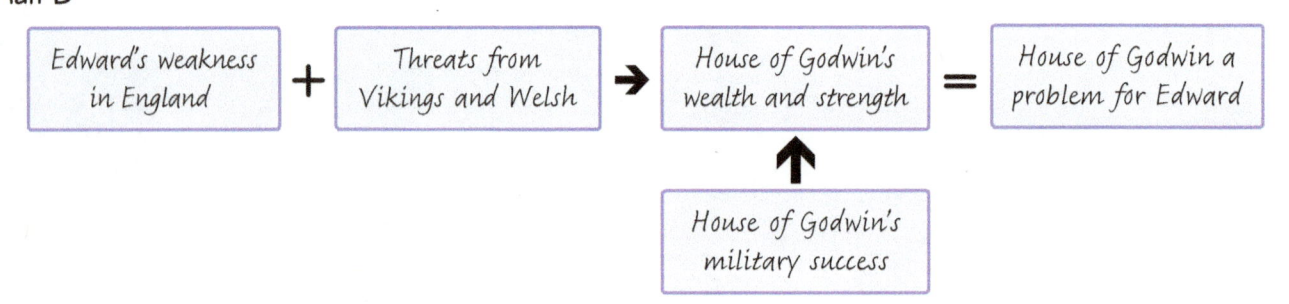

(1) Evaluate ✏ these plans using the table below by writing 'A' or 'B' in the appropriate box.

How well does each plan …	Very well	Quite well	Not at all
show a wide variety of reasons?			
show how one cause leads to another, and so on?			
show how causes interact with each other?			

Remember this?

Edward the Confessor and the House of Godwin

This unit uses the theme of Edward the Confessor and the House of Godwin to build your skills in analysing causation. If you need to review your knowledge of this theme, work through these pages.

1 Circle which of the following statements apply to Edward the Confessor.

- A He was a warrior king.
- B He was a respected lawmaker.
- C He was very religious.
- D His earls obeyed him without question.

2 Circle which of the following were children of Earl Godwin.

- A Robert Curthose
- B Edith
- C Tostig
- D Gyrth

3 Circle which of the following was a significant rival of the Godwins in the 1060s.

- A King Cnut
- B Leofwine of Kent
- C Llewelyn of Wales
- D Aelfgar of Mercia

4 Circle which of the following earldoms belonged to the House of Godwin.

- A Wessex
- B Northumbria
- C Hereford
- D Kent

5 Put these events in the correct order by writing the numbers 1–6 in the boxes beside them.

- A Northumbria rises up against Tostig Godwinson.
- B Death of Edward the Confessor.
- C Harold Godwinson becomes Earl of Wessex.
- D Tostig Godwinson becomes Earl of Northumbria.
- E The Godwins defeat Llewelyn of Wales.
- F Edith, daughter of Earl Godwin, marries Edward the Confessor.

6 Draw lines linking each earl with his earldom. One earldom is used twice.

earl	earldom
A Aelfgar	a Northumbria
B Harold Godwinson	b Kent
C Siward	c Hereford
D Leofwine	d Mercia
E Gyrth	e East Anglia
F Tostig	

Unit 3 Analysing causation

Remember this?

7 For each group below, circle (A) the odd one out and write (✎) why it is the odd one out.

a | Leofwine | Siward | Wulfnoth | Harold |
....

b | Danelaw | Siward | Harold Godwinson | Tostig |
....

c | assassination of rivals | false accusations to take money and land | forging silver pennies | not retaliating against Malcolm III |
....

d | making laws | advising the king | appointing bishops | overseeing justice |
....

8 How did the Godwins get influence over the Church? (✎) ....
....
....

9 Who was Tostig Godwinson's wife? (✎) ....

10 The following statements are all incorrect. Write (✎) the correct version underneath.

a | Siward replaced Tostig as Earl of Northumbria. |
....

b | Harold led Edward's army against his brother, Tostig. |
....

c | By the 1060s the Godwins controlled half of England. |
....

d | The Vikings were no longer a threat to England under Edward the Confessor. |
....

e | In 1062 Llewelyn and Tostig attacked Edward the Confessor. |
....

f | In 1062 Harold Godwinson led a fleet against the Normans. |
....

24   Unit 3 Analysing causation

Skills boost

1 How do I build a causal argument?

Causal arguments look at series of causes that build up to bring about a specific problem or situation. This skills boost will help you to build a causal argument.

Here are some evidence cards concerning why the House of Godwin became a problem for Edward the Confessor.

- **A** Threats from Vikings, the Welsh
- **B** Harold's military success against Llewelyn
- **C** Wessex was Harold's powerbase
- **D** Harold installed puppet king in Wales
- **L** House of Godwin's huge military resources
- **E** Northumbria was Tostig's powerbase
- **K** Edward's influence in Danelaw was limited
- **F** Edward himself: religious, not a warrior, not strong
- **J** Edward needed House of Godwin's support
- **I** Earls ignored Edward over Northumbrian rebellion
- **H** Northumbria rebelled against Tostig
- **G** Edward gave Godwins earldoms across England

Why was the House of Godwin a problem for Edward the Confessor?

1 a Pick any three from cards A–L and write them in column 2 of the table.

1 Caused by…	2 Card chosen	Resulting in …
		The House of Godwin being a problem for Edward the Confessor

b Identify any cards that caused your three choices. Write them in column 1 (Caused by …). If one of your choices does not have any causes, leave the cell beside it in column 1 blank.

2 Causal arguments must be made in a logical order, showing how one cause led to another until the outcome was reached. Using the evidence cards above, complete these two flow diagrams to make a logical sequence of causation.

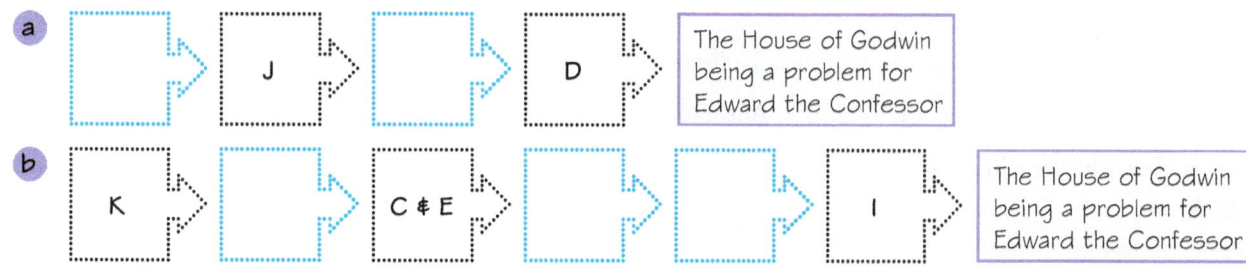

a ☐ → J → ☐ → D → The House of Godwin being a problem for Edward the Confessor

b K → C & E → ☐ → ☐ → I → The House of Godwin being a problem for Edward the Confessor

Unit 3 Analysing causation 25

Skills boost

2 How do I develop a causal argument?

When you write causal arguments, it is important to avoid making them read like lists. This skills boost will help you to write developed causal arguments.

Students were asked to use the flow diagram below to write two paragraphs explaining why the House of Godwin was a problem for Edward the Confessor.

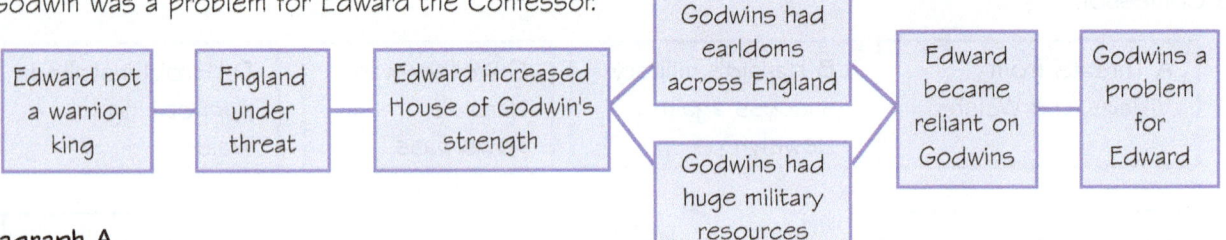

Edward not a warrior king → England under threat → Edward increased House of Godwin's strength → Godwins had earldoms across England / Godwins had huge military resources → Edward became reliant on Godwins → Godwins a problem for Edward

Paragraph A

Members of the House of Godwin were given earldoms across England and consequently became militarily strong. There was a family tie because Edward married Edith. Wessex was important for England's defence. This caused Edward to rely on Harold Godwinson.

Paragraph B

Secondly, the threat from Wales led to the House of Godwin becoming stronger still. Tostig and Harold joined together to defeat Llewelyn in 1062. This resulted in the Welsh being much less of a threat to Edward, but it led Harold to assume the role of sub-regulus and in turn appoint his own puppet king to lead Wales. The consequence of this was that Edward had been sidelined by Harold.

(1) In paragraphs A and B, circle (A) the words and phrases used to build a causal argument.

> **Words and phrases used to build causal arguments**
> caused   because   consequently/consequence of
> in turn   leading/led to   resulted in

(2) What are the strengths and weaknesses of the two paragraphs? Complete the table below with the appropriate paragraph letter.

Strengths	A, B or both?	Weaknesses	A, B or both?
Clear focus to the paragraph		Paragraph focus uncertain	
Causation is explained		A series of statements about cause	
Specific supporting evidence		Undeveloped historical knowledge	

An important part of developing a causal argument is supporting it with evidence.

(3) Using some of the linking phrases from (1) and your own words, complete the paragraph below.

Edward was a weak king .... his religious, peaceable nature was not suited to medieval kingship, which .... to rely on the big earldoms' military forces. ...., the likes of Harold and Tostig developed their own powerbases in Wessex and Northumbria, ... them being more powerful than Edward. The Godwinson victory over Llewelyn in 1062 is a fine example of that. It .... Harold to appoint a new king who was his puppet, ... making Harold Edward's effective sub-regulus and .... undermining Edward.

Skills boost

3 How do I link causal arguments to the question?

Linking causal arguments back to the question is important to make sure you don't wander from the question focus. This skills boost will help you understand how to do that.

It is important to develop a chain of causes from your start point to your end point and stay focused. Look at this list of factors that could be included in the answer to the question on page 21.

A Vikings were a major threat	B Victory over Llewelyn	C House of Godwin = ambitious
D Earls ignored Edward and followed Harold over Northumbrian revolt	E Edward needed support of powerful earls	F House of Godwin much more powerful than Edward
G Harold given Wessex, Hereford, so was most powerful earl of all	H Harold installed his own puppet king in Wales	I Harold effectively made himself Edward's sub-regulus
J Edward was a weak king	K Tostig abused his power	L Godwinsons' military power
M Northumbria revolted in 1065	N Edward attacked Llewelyn in 1062	O Tostig = Earl of Northumbria

Using the factors listed above, the flow chart below shows a paragraph plan to explain one way that Edward being a weak king led to the House of Godwin becoming much more powerful than he was.

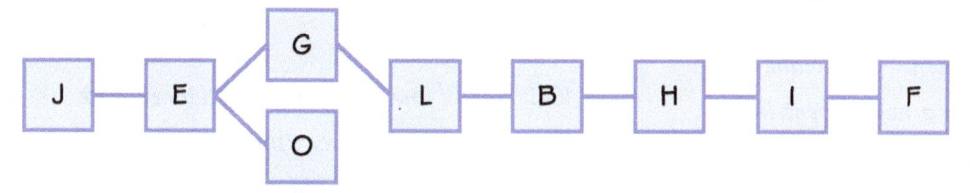

J → E → (G, O) → L → B → H → I → F

> There may be many possible factors leading to an event. Ranking them by importance will ensure you select the ones that you can explain most effectively.

(1) Study the evidence below, then underline (A) three factors in the list above that you think had the greatest impact on the House of Godwin becoming much more powerful than Edward.

> Harold turned on Tostig, who lost and was exiled. Tostig had been Harold's main rival for power.

> Edward had no children of his own so Harold and Tostig were rivals to replace him.

(2) Put ✏ your underlined causes in order of importance, according to how effectively you think you can explain them.

A student using the paragraph plan above has decided that one reason for the House of Godwin being a problem for Edward the Confessor was the threat from Wales. At the end of their analysis, they need to link back to the question to explain why. Having ranked the factors by importance and chosen those with the greatest impact, they need an effective final sentence that:

- summarises the chain of causes
- ends the chain with the key ideas/words from the question.

(3) Tick ✓ which of the following final sentences best links the causal argument back to the question on page 21.

| A | So, Edward's weakness led him to make powerful earls, giving the House of Godwin military power that won victory over Llewelyn. This enabled Harold to install a puppet king in Wales, and then he became sub-regulus, so the House of Godwin became more powerful than Edward. | ☐ |
| B | So, weak Edward needed the support of powerful earldoms. He favoured the House of Godwin, which resulted in Harold Godwinson controlling Wales and ultimately becoming more powerful than the English king. | ☐ |

Sample response

Get back on track

Careful planning is important to ensure that you produce an effective causal argument with a clear progression towards your final explanation of the issue in the question.

Study the plans below that students have written in response to the exam-style question on page 21.

Plan A: Paragraph 1:

Edward the Confessor's weakness led to:

(a) Building up powerful earls to provide support and defence ➔ Harold Earl of Wessex and Hereford and Tostig ➔ Earl of Northumbria ➔ built up wealth, military strength

(b) And at same time as Edward the Confessor's weakness ➔ threat to England from Wales and the Vikings grew greater.

Paragraph 2:

1062 Llewelyn defeated by Harold's and Tostig's military forces. Harold's ambition = important cause too ➔ Harold appointing a new puppet king whom he could control ➔ assuming role of Edward's sub-regulus ➔ Edward's weakness being reinforced.

Paragraph 3:

Edward's weakness in the North also an **important cause** because of Danelaw and Viking threat ➔ Tostig Earl of Northumbria abusing his power ➔ rebellion ➔ Harold undermining Edward further by leading the other earls in ignoring Edward ➔ Edward's weakness being reinforced. Also exile of Tostig ➔ Harold more powerful by getting rid of a possible rival to the throne; Edward no heirs so Harold now in strong position, Edward reliant on him – feeding his ambition ➔ Edward's weakness clear.

Plan B: Paragraph 1:

Edward the Confessor was weak king: religious, peaceable, no children (heirs).

Paragraph 2:

Edward tried to build up support ➔ making powerful earls ➔ Harold Earl of Wessex and Hereford and Tostig ➔ Northumbria.

Paragraph 3:

Edward the Confessor's weakness ➔ threat from Vikings and Welsh more serious.

Paragraph 4:

1062 Harold and Tostig defeated Llewelyn ➔ Harold installing puppet king whom he could control ➔ him assuming role of Edward's sub-regulus.

Paragraph 5:

Tostig's abuse of power in Northumbria ➔ rebellion 1065 ➔ Harold leading earls putting it down ➔ undermining Edward.

Paragraph 6:

Tostig ➔ exile ➔ Harold having no rival for his aim to take the throne after Edward died.

To develop a causal argument, you need to:
- clearly show causation
- combine causation with evidence
- link back to the question
- highlight other important causes.

(1) Which do you think is the better plan and why?

....
....
....
....

Unit 3 Analysing causation

Your turn!

Get back on track

Now it's your turn to try and answer an exam-style question.

Exam-style question

Explain why the House of Godwin was a problem for Edward the Confessor.

You may use the following in your answer:

- Tostig
- Wessex

You **must** also include information of your own. (12 marks)

1. Use the words and phrases from page 26 to write one of the paragraphs from plan A on page 28.

Remember to use factual evidence to develop and support your argument.

Unit 3 Analysing causation 29

Review your skills

Check up

Review your response to the exam-style question on page 29. Tick ✓ the column to show how well you think you have done each of the following.

	Had a go ✓	Nearly there ✓	Got it! ✓
built a causal argument	☐	☐	☐
developed the causal argument effectively	☐	☐	☐
linked the causal argument to the question	☐	☐	☐

Look over all of your work in this unit. Note down three things you have learned that you will apply when analysing causation.

1 ....
2 ....
3 ....

Need more practice?

On separate paper, plan and write your response to the exam-style question below.

> **Exam-style question**
>
> Explain why Edwin and Morcar's rebellion in 1068 failed.
>
> You may use the following in your answer:
> - Edgar Aethling
> - the Marcher earls
>
> You **must** also use information of your own. (12 marks)

How confident do you feel about each of these **skills**? Colour in the bars.

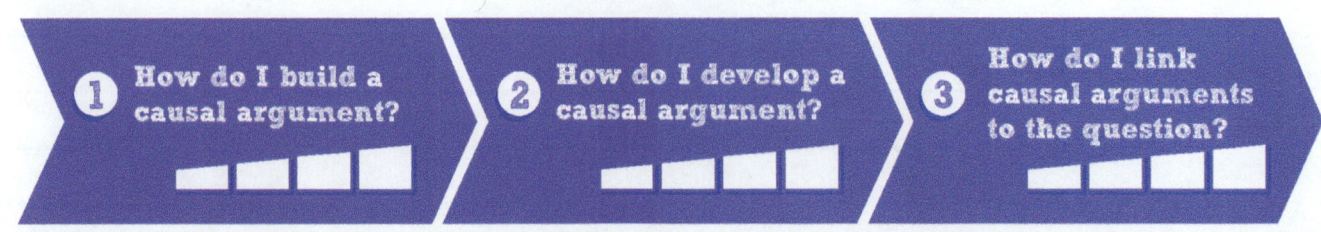

1 How do I build a causal argument?

2 How do I develop a causal argument?

3 How do I link causal arguments to the question?

Get started

④ Evaluating cause in context

Understanding cause requires understanding its context. This unit will help you to evaluate change in context. The skills you will build are how to:

- identify the features of context that are relevant
- show the influence of context
- evaluate the importance of context.

In the exam, you will be asked to tackle questions such as the one below. This unit will prepare you to write your own response to this type of question.

> **Exam-style question**
>
> 'The main reason the Anglo-Saxons stopped rebelling against William I was because the Danes stopped supporting them.'
>
> How far do you agree? Explain your answer.
>
> You may use the following in your answer:
>
> - Hereward the Wake
> - Norman sheriffs
>
> You **must** also use information of your own. (16 marks)

What is context?

Context can be defined as the circumstances or setting in which events happen. Events can have a political, economic, social or religious context, for example, as well as an international and domestic context.

The three key questions in the **skills boosts** will help you understand how to evaluate cause in context.

| 1 How do I identify the features of context that are relevant? | 2 How do I show the influence of context? | 3 How do I evaluate the importance of context? |

Get started

Being able to describe the context in which historical figures acted and against which historical events took place can be very helpful in explaining why people reacted in a certain way or why circumstances changed in the way that they did.

1 Draw lines linking the contexts (situations) and the terms that could be applied to describe them.

For example: **B** economics → **c** (growth, boom, recession, downturn) or **A** politics → **b** (extremist, moderate) and **d** (conservative, radical)

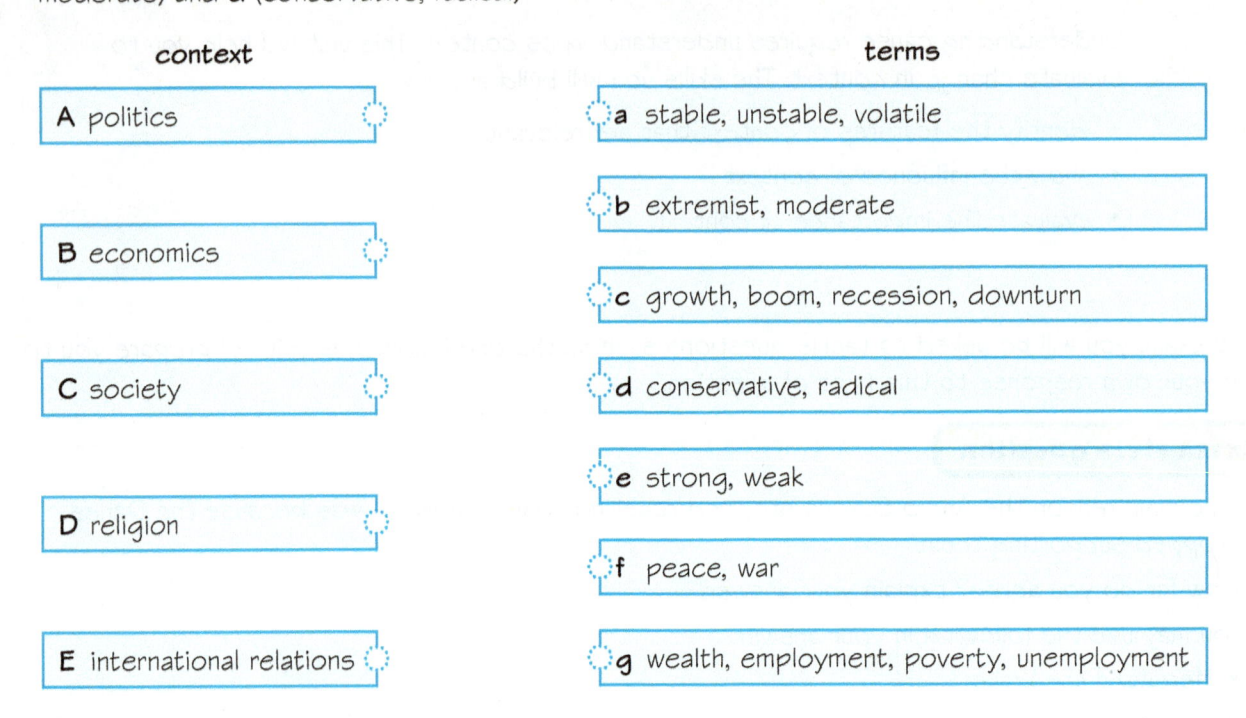

context	terms
A politics	a stable, unstable, volatile
	b extremist, moderate
B economics	c growth, boom, recession, downturn
C society	d conservative, radical
	e strong, weak
D religion	f peace, war
E international relations	g wealth, employment, poverty, unemployment

It is also possible to make predictions about what outcomes might result from a specific context.

2 Draw lines to match each context to its possible outcomes.

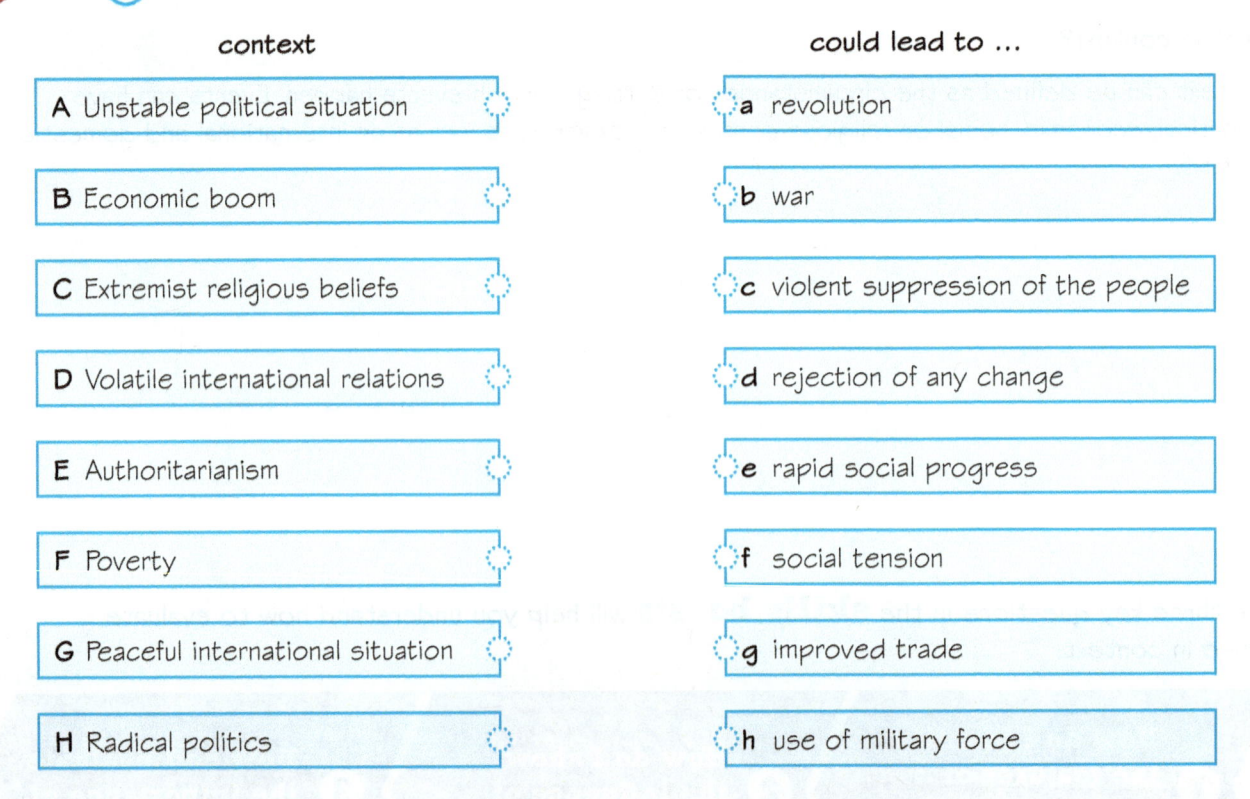

context	could lead to …
A Unstable political situation	a revolution
B Economic boom	b war
C Extremist religious beliefs	c violent suppression of the people
D Volatile international relations	d rejection of any change
E Authoritarianism	e rapid social progress
F Poverty	f social tension
G Peaceful international situation	g improved trade
H Radical politics	h use of military force

Unit 4 Evaluating cause in context

Anglo-Saxon resistance to Norman rule

Remember this?

This unit uses the theme of Anglo-Saxon resistance to Norman rule to build your skills in evaluating cause in context. If you need to review your knowledge of this theme, work through these pages.

1. Write the letter of the following events against the correct dates in the chronological list below.

   A Hereward, the Danes and Morcar join forces against the Normans
   B The Danes join Edgar Aethling and attack York
   C Uprising in York after Robert Cumin killed in Durham
   D Norman earls join with Anglo-Saxon Waltheof against William
   E Edwin and Morcar's revolt
   F Submission of the earls
   G Herefordshire attacked by the Welsh and Eadric the Wild
   H The Harrying of the North

   1066 .... 1067 .... 1068 ....
   1069 (February) .... 1069 (September) ....
   1069–70 .... 1070–71 .... 1075 ....

2. Find and circle the answers to clues **a** to **l** in the word search below.

   ```
   O D F I V E F Q I E
   H D M V E W I K H D
   E F O R T N T I C G
   R O R A S B Z N O A
   E L C W A B O G I R
   F E A E W E S S E X
   O F R E L U B W A E
   R O G R L Y E E D A
   D U R H A M R Y W R
   X G E L D F N N A I
   ```

   a. Bishop of Bayeux, involved in land-grabs when acting as regent for William in 1067. ....
   b. Earl who submitted to William, rebelled in 1068 and later joined Hereward the Wake. ....
   c. Place where Robert Cumin was killed by rebels. ....
   d. 60 per cent of Yorkshire was classified as this after the Harrying of the North. ....
   e. Percentage of land still held by Anglo-Saxon aristocrats by 1087. ....
   f. Led the Danish fleet that supported Hereward the Wake. ....
   g. Another leading Norman involved in land-grabs (surname only). ....
   h. Heavy tax levied by William in December 1066, a cause of the 1068 rebellion. ....
   i. Isolated East Anglian place where Morcar was captured in 1071. ....
   j. Roger de Breteuil, Earl of ...., rebelled against William in 1075.
   k. Richest earldom in England, kept by William for himself. ....
   l. The Aethling; attacked the north of England, backed by Malcolm III of Scotland. ....

Unit 4 Evaluating cause in context

Remember this?

3 The following statements are incorrect. Write ✎ the correct version underneath each one.

　a William secured the south of England by negotiating terms with the Anglo-Saxons.
　...

　b William passed an Act of Parliament to take all of England into his ownership.
　...

　c Building castles was William's way of protecting his men.
　...

　d Under William, sheriffs were answerable to the earls.
　...

　e The Danes left England in the autumn of 1069 because William's army defeated them.
　...

　f The 1069 rebellions were confined to the north-east of England.
　...

4 Circle Ⓐ which of the following were earls of Northumbria.

| A | Robert Cumin | B | Gospatric |
| C | Edwin | D | Waltheof |

5 Circle Ⓐ the location of the Anglo-Saxon rebels' base in 1070–71.

| A | Peterborough | B | Durham |
| C | York | D | Ely |

6 Circle Ⓐ which of the following were involved in the 1075 rebellion.

| A | Wulfstan | B | Roger de Gael |
| C | Waltheof | D | Odo |

7 Circle Ⓐ which of the following was **not** a reason for the 1075 revolt.

| A | Anglo-Saxon rebelliousness | B | The death of Edwin |
| C | William's absence | D | Powerful Danish allies |

8 Tick ✓ whether the statements below are true or false.　　　true　false

　a Morcar was executed for his part in the 1070–71 rebellion.　□　□

　b At first, William was keen to be seen to uphold Anglo-Saxon laws and traditions.　□　□

Unit 4 Evaluating cause in context

Skills boost

1. How do I identify the features of context that are relevant?

Context can help to explain why the same person reacts to the same problem in different ways at different times. A difference in the situation, or in the events leading up to it, can produce different outcomes. This skills boost will help you identify the relevant features of context.

Look back to the exam-style question on page 31. Why did Anglo-Saxon rebellion stop after 1071? Why not sooner? Why did it not continue, since William I's approach to ruling England and the Anglo-Saxons did not change?

A student made the following notes:

Political context 1066	1068	Post-1071
There were both Norman and Anglo-Saxon earls	No change	
Anglo-Saxon earls submitted to William	Several earls rebelled	
William brought southern England firmly under his control	No change	
Fortified burhs protected the people	Changing: Norman castles being built	
Religious context 1066	1069	Post-1071
Anglo-Saxon clergy remained in place	No change	
The Danish threat 1066	1069	Post-1071
William's concern about Danish intervention in, and raids on, England	No change	
Northern England harder to govern, heavily influenced by Danelaw	No change	

(1) Think about the following events:

- rebellions 1068 (Edwin, Morcar), 1069 (Edgar, Danes; in northern England), 1070–71 (Hereward, Morcar, Danes; in East Anglia)
- the Harrying of the North, 1069–70
- Stigand replaced by Lanfranc as Archbishop of Canterbury, 1070
- William replaced Anglo-Saxons with Normans in Mercia, East Anglia, the North, 1071

Did they cause the context to change after 1071? How? Complete ✏️ the table for post-1071.

(2) Why had the Anglo-Saxons stopped rebelling after 1071? Use the changes in context in your completed table to inform your answer. ✏️

....
....
....

Unit 4 Evaluating cause in context

Skills boost

2 How do I show the influence of context?

If you are looking to explain an event, remember to consider context alongside the other causes. Does it change? Has it influenced other developments leading to the event? This skills boost will help you to show the influence of context.

The notes below were made by a student looking at why the Anglo-Saxons stopped rebelling against William I. Her notes focus on reviewing developments in the situation: how William's reactions to rebellions and treatment of Anglo-Saxons changed.

- 1066: William kept some Anglo-Saxon earls; Church posts still in Anglo-Saxon hands, but sheriffs replaced by William's men.
- 1068: Morcar and Edwin's rebellion defeated, they're pardoned.
- 1069–70: rebellions in the north-east, Welsh Marches, Devon. Danes and Edgar Aethling attack York. Defeated → Harrying of the North → North laid waste → Danelaw weakened greatly.
- 1070: Anglo-Saxon Church purged; only one Anglo-Saxon bishop left; Normanisation.
- 1070–71: Hereward's rebellion in East Anglia. Morcar, Edwin escape, join him. Defeated. Morcar and Edwin's lands in Mercia, East Anglia, the North are forfeited → given to Normans; William consolidates land → smaller Norman earldoms; thegns leave England or serve Normans.

1 What do you notice about William's treatment of Anglo-Saxons and rebellions?

....

....

2 Review the student's notes above. Beside each date in the table below, write the change in context that was also happening and which may have led to Anglo-Saxon rebellions dying out.

Date	Change in context
1069–70	
1070	
1071	

Now assess how changing context can lead to different events and outcomes, and how that links to the question. Study the student answer extract below and answer **3** to demonstrate this.

> Anglo-Saxon resistance dying out by 1071 cannot be explained by the role of the Danes. Firstly, they only supported the rebellions in 1069 and 1070–71, and only for the spoils. Secondly, the threat of Danish raids against William remained after 1071. Instead, the end of Anglo-Saxon resistance coincides with a changing domestic context. … Thus the domestic context explains the ending of Anglo-Saxon resistance.

3 Write 2–3 sentences that could fill the gap in the student's paragraph above, explaining how the domestic context changed. ....

....

....

Unit 4 Evaluating cause in context

Skills boost

3 How do I evaluate the importance of context?

There will always be a context for events, but it is not always significant. This skills boost will help you to determine the significance of context.

A good way to evaluate the importance of the context of an event is to ask:

> Why did the event happen then? Why not sooner/later? What changed?

1 Use the table to test whether changing context can explain the ending of Anglo-Saxon resistance to William after 1071. For each description of context, tick ✓ whether it was present in 1066 and/or post-1071. If both columns have been ticked, there is no change. If there has been no change, it cannot help explain the decline in Anglo-Saxon rebellion.

Domestic context	1066 ✓	Post-1071 ✓
William wanted to appear to be upholding Anglo-Saxon laws and traditions		
Norman castles had been built across England		
Northern England, Mercia and East Anglia were governed by Norman earls		
The feudal system had been established		
Context of Danish threat	**1066 ✓**	**Post-1071 ✓**
Northern England was heavily influenced by Danelaw, strong links with Danes		
William was concerned about Danish raids/invasions		

2 a You now need to assess the significance of this context. How significant was the domestic context to the ending of Anglo-Saxon resistance after 1071? Write your score and then explain it. Use these scores:

1 = highly significant   2 = very significant   3 = quite significant   4 = not at all significant

Score: ☐ ....

....

b How significant was the context of the Danish threat after 1071? Write your score then explain it.

Score: ☐ ....

....

3 How far does the changing context show the Danes as an important factor in ending Anglo-Saxon resistance? Draw an arrow to show your choice.

100% Danes	Largely Danes	More Danes than context	More context than Danes	Largely context	100% context

4 Write an introduction to the exam-style question on page 31. Write 2–3 sentences, explaining how the change in context led to the decline of Anglo-Saxon resistance. Continue on paper if you need to.

....

....

Sample response

Being able to identify and evaluate context is a useful skill that can help you to explain historical events.

Exam-style question

'The main reason the Anglo-Saxons stopped rebelling against William I was because the Danes stopped supporting them.'

How far do you agree? Explain your answer.

You may use the following in your answer:
- Hereward the Wake
- Norman sheriffs

You **must** also use information of your own. (16 marks)

This extract is from one student's answer to the exam-style question above.

> If the Danes' support had been so important to Anglo-Saxon resistance, then there would not have been attacks by Eadric and the Welsh in 1067, nor the rebellion in 1068, as the Danes took part in neither. The Danes did support Edgar in 1069 and Hereward in 1070–71. It is also true that 1071 marked the end of Anglo-Saxon resistance, and the end of Danish support coincided with it because it was not needed any more.
>
> In 1069–70, the Harrying of the North was a turning point in the political context of England. Instead of winning over the Anglo-Saxon aristocracy, William began replacing them. The Harrying of the North was William's revenge for Anglo-Saxon resistance there; as many as 100,000 people died. In 1071 Edwin and Morcar joined Hereward, forfeiting their lands in Northumbria, Mercia and East Anglia to men loyal to William. William also reduced the size of earldoms and consolidated them, so it was harder for Anglo-Saxons to resist. In 1070 the Church was Normanised, and its posts and lands transferred to Normans. By 1075, political circumstances had changed, so Normans had complete control of England. The 1075 revolt was basically Norman led, as William's changes upset the Norman earls of Hereford and East Anglia. The only Anglo-Saxon earl involved in 1075 was Waltheof of Northumbria; he was executed at Winchester in 1076.

1. a. Double underline (A) where the focus of the question is directly referred to.
   b. Underline (A) any mention of when the context of the end of Anglo-Saxon resistance changed.
   c. Circle (A) any explanation of how context changed.
   d. Draw an asterisk (*) where the importance of context is identified.
   e. Write a sentence to end the second paragraph more effectively.

Your turn!

Get back on track

Now it's your turn to try to answer an exam-style question.

Exam-style question

'The main reason that the Anglo-Saxons stopped rebelling against William I was because the Danes stopped supporting them.'

How far do you agree? Explain your answer.

You may use the following in your answer:
- Hereward the Wake
- Norman sheriffs

You **must** also use information of your own. (16 marks)

1. Write a paragraph on one aspect of the changing domestic context that caused the Anglo-Saxons to stop rebelling. Focus on explaining why it was harder for the Anglo-Saxons to resist.

   You should:
   - answer the question directly (why did the Anglo-Saxons stop rebelling?)
   - explain when and how the changing context affected Anglo-Saxon resistance
   - explain how important context is in understanding why the Anglo-Saxons stopped rebelling.

   Here are a few reminders about the end of Anglo-Saxon rebellion, to help you choose your paragraph focus:
   - **Aristocracy:** after 1070 William began replacing the aristocracy.
   - **Church:** after 1070 the Church was Normanised.
   - **Suppression of resistance:** the Harrying of the North after the rebellions of 1069–70.

Unit 4 Evaluating cause in context

Review your skills

Check up

Review your response to the exam-style question on page 39. Tick ✓ the column to show how well you think you have done each of the following.

	Had a go ✓	Nearly there ✓	Got it! ✓
identified the key features of the context	☐	☐	☐
showed the influence of context	☐	☐	☐
evaluated the importance of context	☐	☐	☐
maintained focus on the question	☐	☐	☐

Look over all of your work in this unit. Note down three things you have learned that you will apply when evaluating cause in context.

① ....
② ....
③ ....

Need more practice?

On separate paper, plan and write your response to the exam-style question below.

Exam-style question

'The most serious problem Edward the Confessor faced in the years 1060–66 was the challenge from Earl Tostig.'

How far do you agree? Explain your answer.

You may use the following in your answer:
- Northumberland
- the House of Godwin

You **must** also use information of your own.

(16 marks)

How confident do you feel about each of these **skills**? Colour in the bars.

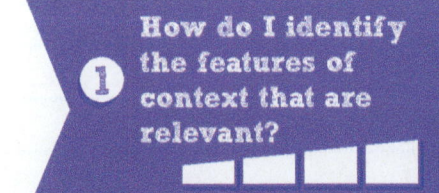

1. How do I identify the features of context that are relevant?
2. How do I show the influence of context?
3. How do I evaluate the importance of context?

Unit 4 Evaluating cause in context

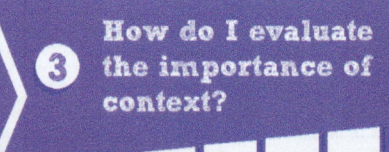

Get started

5 Evaluating significance

This unit will help you to develop the skills to evaluate significance effectively. The skills you will build are how to:

- assess significance
- show that significance can change
- decide what is most significant.

In the exam, you will be asked to tackle questions such as the one below. This unit will prepare you to write your own response to this type of question.

> **Exam-style question**
>
> 'The most significant reason for William's changes to landholding was to crush Anglo-Saxon rebellion.'
>
> How far do you agree? Explain your answer.
>
> You may use the following in your answer:
>
> - forfeiture
> - Marcher earldoms
>
> You **must** also use information of your own. (16 marks)

There are several things that can help you decide if something is significant, including:

? **frequency** – how often it happened; are there lots of examples of it?

? **quantity** – how many people it affected; how widespread it was, socially and geographically

? **quality** – how deeply it was felt by people

? **longevity** – how long it lasted

It is very important to deal with the stated feature, consequence, factor or problem first when answering an essay question, even if you do not think it is the most significant. In the question above, 'to crush Anglo-Saxon rebellion' is the stated problem for you to evaluate.

It is also important to consider relative significance, by comparing the significance of different problems, features, causes or consequences. Here are some useful words and phrases you can use to do this:

| Although X was significant, Y was more so because … | By 10nn, X was becoming more significant than Y because … |

| However, X was more important than Y in such and such a place … | The most significant problem/factor/consequence overall was … |

The three key questions in the **skills boosts** will help you understand how to evaluate significance.

① How do I assess significance?

② How do I show that significance can change?

③ How do I decide what is most significant?

Unit 5 Evaluating significance 41

Get started

A student studying the question on page 41 collected the following pieces of evidence:

> A The feudal system secured payments (rents, taxes, obligations) in return for land.
>
> B William punished rebellion (e.g. Edwin and Morcar 1071), rewarded loyalty (e.g. Odo 1066).
>
> C Land = status, power, wealth; so William controlled his vassals by granting or taking land.
>
> D William's royal forests were an important source of income for him.
>
> E The Marcher earldoms were established to protect England's Welsh border.
>
> F Under the feudal system, tenants-in-chief could dispossess disloyal or rebellious thegns.
>
> G By 1087, less than 5 per cent of land was held by Anglo-Saxon aristocrats.
>
> H By 1087, almost all Anglo-Saxon thegns had Norman lords, making them less of a threat.
>
> I Castle-building in strategic locations often led to Anglo-Saxon homes being demolished.
>
> J Consolidating and reducing the size of earldoms after 1071 made them easier to defend.

1 Look at the evidence in the student's list and sort it into the three columns in the table below.

Evidence of economic gain as a reason	Evidence of defence as a reason	Evidence of political power as a reason

2 a Which column in **1** had the most evidence? ....

b How far do you agree that this was the most important reason why William changed landholding in England? Circle your choice.

| Very little | Partly | Largely | Strongly |

3 The student looked at the evidence in the list that suggested economic gain as a cause. Which piece of evidence has a very strong link between economic gain as a cause and political power?

....

4 Look at your answer to **3**. Which other pieces of evidence from the list can be linked to that piece?

....

5 Now you have considered the evidence in more detail, look back at your answer to question **2**. Have you changed your mind? Circle your choice and explain your decision.

| Very little | Partly | Largely | Strongly |

....
....
....
....

Unit 5 Evaluating significance

Changes to landholding

This unit uses the theme of changes to landholding to build your skills in evaluating significance. If you need to review your knowledge of this theme, work through these pages.

1 Draw lines linking the terms to the correct definition.

term	definition
A Relief	a Payment made by Anglo-Saxons to the king, to allow them to keep their land
B Redemption	b Losing something as punishment for a crime or bad action
C Motte	c Devastating or laying waste to
D Castellan	d Mound of earth with a keep on top
E Harrying	e Payment made to the king before an heir inherited land
F Forfeiting	f Governor of a castle and its surrounding territory

2 Tick whether the following statements are true or false.

		true	false
a	At first, William was keen to be seen to uphold Anglo-Saxon traditions and laws.	☐	☐
b	The Anglo-Saxon Church was purged in 1070.	☐	☐
c	After the purge of the Anglo-Saxon Church there were no Anglo-Saxon bishops.	☐	☐
d	Edwin and Morcar forfeited their lands in 1068.	☐	☐
e	Waltheof was a Marcher earl.	☐	☐
f	Anglo-Saxon thegn Eadric joined with the Danes to attack England in 1067.	☐	☐

3 Number the following events 1–6 to show the order in which they happened.

A Edwin and Morcar's rebellion
B Harrying of the North
C Edgar and the Danes attack York
D Submission of the earls
E Building of Norman castles gets underway
F Hereward flees Ely and disappears

Unit 5 Evaluating significance 43

4 The following statements all contain mistakes. Write ✏️ the correct version underneath each one.

a | By 1087 there were only five Anglo-Saxon tenants-in-chief.

b | Norman castellans were notorious for corruptly seizing land.

c | If Anglo-Saxon landholders wanted to keep using their own land they had to pay relief.

d | The land of landholders who died without heirs was given to the Church.

e | After 1071 William made sure his landholders' land was spread across England.

f | Under the feudal system thegns could only be dispossessed by the king.

5 Circle Ⓐ your answers to the questions below. Some may have more than one answer.

a | Which of the following was Earl of Kent after 1066?
  - A | William
  - B | FitzOsbern
  - C | Odo
  - D | Morcar

b | Which of the following were payments based on landholding?
  - A | Geld
  - B | Redeeming
  - C | Hides
  - D | Reliefs

c | How much land did the Church hold?
  - A | 20 per cent
  - B | 25 per cent
  - C | 30 per cent
  - D | 35 per cent

d | How much land did William keep as royal demesne?
  - A | 20 per cent
  - B | 25 per cent
  - C | 30 per cent
  - D | 35 per cent

e | Which of the following could be part of a knight's duties?
  - A | Building castles
  - B | Being lord of a manor
  - C | Protecting his lord's lands
  - D | Overseeing justice in manor courts

Unit 5 Evaluating significance

Skills boost

1 How do I assess significance?

'How far' questions require you to judge what was the most important (significant) problem, feature, change, cause or consequence. Having more pieces of evidence to support it doesn't necessarily make something the most significant. This skills boost will help you to assess significance. (For more on judgements, see Unit 7.)

A student trying to establish the most significant reason for changes in landholding under William I collected the following evidence:

A The feudal system provided William with free annual knight service and an army.
B Changes in landholding → more revenues, e.g. relief, rents.
C When William became king he declared all land was his to keep (for revenue) or grant to (to reward loyalty) or confiscate from (to punish) his subjects.
D New Marcher earldoms protected England's Welsh borders.
E Anglo-Saxons had to pay to redeem their own lands from William.
F Strategically important land was taken for castles.
G Forest laws had high fines, giving William more revenues.
H In 1070 the Normanisation of the Church led to a massive change in landholding.
I Under the feudal system, tenants-in-chief could dispossess rebellious thegns.

1) In the table, write the letter of each piece of evidence, from the student's list above, that goes with each category. Some pieces of evidence might belong in more than one column.

Reason	Strong government	Defence	Revenues	Crush Anglo-Saxon resistance
Evidence				

2) One way to assess significance is to look at the quantity of evidence. Given that, which factor do you think was most significant? ....

Another way to decide if something was significant is to consider how things would have been different without it.

3) Could William have succeeded in staying King of England if D, F or I had not happened? Complete ✓ the table, then pick one and explain your choice.

	Yes, probably ✓	Maybe ✓	No way ✓
D			
F			
I			

....

4) If you could pick just one change to landholding from the list that would have the greatest impact on William being able to stay King of England, which would it be and why?

....
....

5) a Has your answer to 2 changed? ....
   b Which is the more effective way to test signficance: by considering quantity or impact?

....

Unit 5 Evaluating significance 45

2 How do I show that significance can change?

What is significant can vary, for example with time and place. It can also vary with question focus. This skills boost will help you to compare significance.

A student working on the question of which reasons were most significant for William's changes to landholding researched the following evidence about William's decisions on landholding before 1070.

- William was keen to present himself as keeping to Anglo-Saxon law and traditions.
- Anglo-Saxon earls still held a lot of land, especially in Mercia, East Anglia and the North.
- William, Odo, FitzOsbern held land in the strategic south and south-east.
- William established new Marcher earldoms with greater powers than other earldoms.

1 Look at the table below. In order to show that significance can change, look at the situation after 1070 then place a tick ✓ in the last column if it had also been the case before 1070.

Situation after 1070	Before 1070? ✓
William focused more on practical solutions for maintaining control	
Harrying of the North → William replaces Anglo-Saxon aristocracy there	
Normanisation of the Church: all but one bishop was Norman	
William, Odo, FitzOsbern held land in the strategic south and south-east	
Marcher earls had the same powers and obligations as other earls	
Size of earldoms generally reduced, including Norman earldoms	

2 What was the most significant reason behind the changes to William's approach to landholding after 1070? Explain ✏️ your choice.

   a Before 1070 ....

   b From 1070 onwards ....

3 Write ✏️ 2–3 sentences to explain whether crushing Anglo-Saxon resistance was always the most important reason behind William's changes to landholding. You should show that significance can change.

....

....

....

....

....

....

Skills boost

3 How do I decide what is most significant?

Sometimes the question suggests what is most significant. Be prepared to challenge the question. This skills boost will help you to decide what is most significant in the question of whether increasing Crown revenues was the main way that William increased his control of England in the years 1066–71.

Increasing Crown revenues	Crushing Anglo-Saxon resistance
Actions: took 20 per cent of England for himself; introduced royal forest, with harsh laws that made extra revenues in fines	**Actions:** Resistance in 1067, 1068, 1069, 1070–71 led to reducing size of earldoms after 1070–71

1. The table above shows details of increasing Crown revenues and crushing Anglo-Saxon resistance. In order to compare significance, look at the actions William took to achieve them. Which had the biggest impact on William's control of England? ....

One way of deciding the significance of a cause, consequence or change is to look at its interaction with other causes, consequences or changes. Study these four factors in one student's notes on William's attempts to secure a grip on England.

A <u>Encourage loyalty with land.</u> Loyalty was vital. William gave key Normans like Odo and FitzOsbern rich lands in the strategically important south and south-east, for example.

B <u>Increase Crown revenues.</u> Keeping 20 per cent of England and introducing forest was important.

C <u>Defend England's borders.</u> Where were the most important areas? The borders with Wales and Scotland, and the south-east and eastern coasts (Danes). Marcher earldoms were given more powers and privileges initially, including not paying taxes, although this changed later.

D <u>Crush Anglo-Saxon resistance.</u> Resistance often focused on the North and later East Anglia. This could be costly. William needed men he could trust in those areas.

2. a Consider which was the most significant way William increased his control by looking at the impact of each on the others. Did A have a knock-on effect on B? C? D? Briefly explain any knock-on effects below. If there are none, leave the answer line blank. Two have been done to help you.

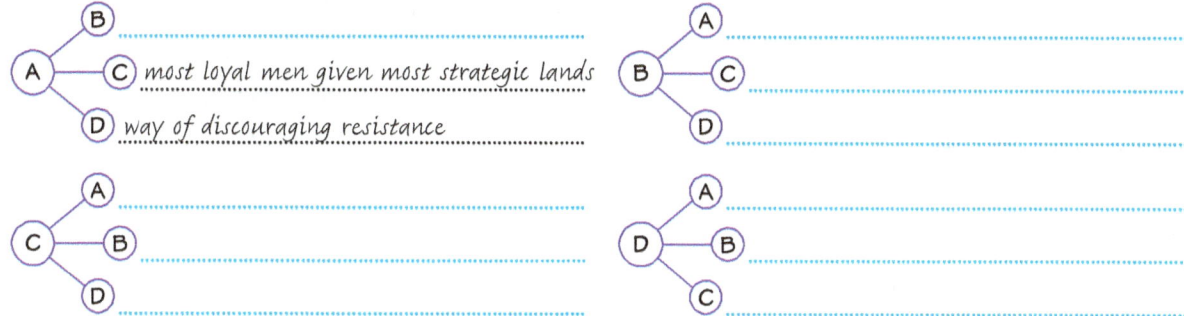

   A—B .... A—B ....
   A—C most loyal men given most strategic lands   B—C ....
   A—D way of discouraging resistance   B—D ....

   C—A ....   D—A ....
   C—B ....   D—B ....
   C—D ....   D—C ....

   b Look at your answers for 2 a. Which way(s) are most important (interact(s) most with other ways)? ....

> **Remember:**
> - Significance is not necessarily based on how much evidence there is.
> - What is significant can change with time and context.
> - What is significant can be determined by its impact on or interaction with other developments.

Unit 5 Evaluating significance

Sample response

Exam-style question

'The most important reason for William's changes to landholding was to crush Anglo-Saxon rebellion.'

How far do you agree? Explain your answer.

Here are three students' responses to the exam-style question above.

Answer A

Crushing Anglo-Saxon resistance was quite a significant reason behind changes in landholding in William I's reign. After the Harrying of the North, the Danelaw was greatly weakened. Later William made earldoms smaller (including Norman ones) and consolidated them, making them easier to defend. At first, William wanted to support Anglo-Saxon traditions and laws. This explains why he allowed Edwin and Morcar to keep their lands after 1068, so this could be quite a significant reason in explaining landholding too.

Answer B

Crushing Anglo-Saxon resistance is the most significant reason for changes in landholding throughout William's reign. It was important for a new, Norman king. There was resistance from the start. Sometimes this involved the Danes, like in 1069, or the Welsh (1067). England's borders needed protecting. Border areas could be vulnerable to rebellion. This is why the Marcher earldoms were established. If the borders were protected then it would make rebellion harder. So, protecting England's borders was the most significant reason for the changes in landholding throughout William's reign. This is why William kept land in the south and gave Odo Kent. Anglo-Saxon resistance died out after 1071, so protecting borders was important.

Answer C

Crushing resistance – Anglo-Saxon and Norman – was the most significant reason behind changes in landholding after 1070. Having laid waste to the North in 1069–70, William began replacing Anglo-Saxon landholders with Normans. In the early years of his reign, he had tried to show he was supportive of Anglo-Saxon traditions and laws. He even pardoned Edwin and Morcar after the 1068 rebellion. After 1071 he took their lands and gave more land to Normans. After 1071 there was no Anglo-Saxon rebellion, but in 1075 Norman earls led one. From 1071 William had begun reducing the size of earldoms and consolidating landholdings, making them easier to defend. He also reduced the powers of the Marcher earls. This shows that although crushing resistance was key to changes in landholding, crushing Anglo-Saxon resistance was no longer the driving reason after 1071.

1. Read the students' responses and complete ✓ the table to highlight the strengths of each.

Has the answer …	A	B	C
clearly highlighted the most significant cause?			
supported it with specific evidence?			
shown how it impacted on other factors?			
shown any change of significant factor over time?			

Your turn!

Get back on track

Now it's your turn to try to answer an exam-style question.

Exam-style question

'Reducing the power of the earls was the most significant reason behind changes in landholding under William I.'

How far do you agree? Explain your answer.

You may use the following in your answer:
- forfeiture
- Marcher earldoms

You **must** also use information of your own.

(16 marks)

1. Draw up a plan for an answer to the question above.

2. Write the introduction and conclusion to go with your plan. The introduction must be clear about how far you think reducing the power of the earls was the most significant reason behind changes in landholding, and also identify other reasons and how important they were. Your conclusion must summarise the main points of your plan and show how far you agree with the statement in the question. Continue on a separate piece of paper if you need to.

Unit 5 Evaluating significance

Review your skills

Check up

Review your response to the exam-style question on page 49. Tick ✓ the column to show how well you think you have done each of the following.

	Had a go ✓	Nearly there ✓	Got it! ✓
identified what was significant	☐	☐	☐
showed how significance changed over time	☐	☐	☐
showed what was most significant	☐	☐	☐
supported my points with evidence	☐	☐	☐

Look over all of your work in this unit. Note down three things you have learned that you will apply when evaluating significance.

1. ....
2. ....
3. ....

Need more practice?

On separate paper, plan and write your response to the exam-style question below.

Exam-style question

'The most significant threat to William I's rule in the years 1066–71 was Edgar Aethling.'

How far do you agree? Explain your answer.

You may use the following in your answer:
- claim to the throne
- Anglo-Saxon earls

You **must** also use information of your own.

(16 marks)

How confident do you feel about each of these **skills**? Colour in the bars.

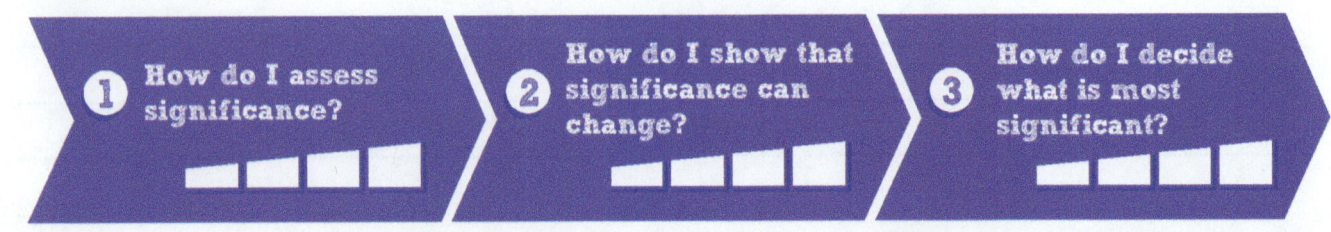

1. How do I assess significance?
2. How do I show that significance can change?
3. How do I decide what is most significant?

Unit 5 Evaluating significance

Get started

6 Evaluating consequence

Students answering questions involving consequence often wander off focus. Essays on consequence must analyse results or effects and their impact, ensuring their relevance to the points in the question. This unit will help you to develop the skills to evaluate consequence effectively. The skills you will build are how to:

- identify consequences
- show how/why something is a consequence
- decide on the main consequence.

In the exam, you will be asked to tackle questions such as the one below. This unit will prepare you to write your own response to this type of question.

> **Exam-style question**
>
> 'The main consequence of the Harrying of the North was the destruction of crops and farming land.'
>
> How far do you agree? Explain your answer.
>
> You may use the following in your answer:
>
> - wasteland
> - Vikings
>
> You **must** also use information of your own. (16 marks)

Types of consequence

As well as being political, economic, social or religious, for example, consequences can be immediate, short-term or long-term. Sometimes the most significant consequences are only realised a long time after the events that led to them happened.

Consequences can also be intended or unintended. Intended consequences are anticipated when actions are planned. However, even the best-laid plans can have surprise results. These are unintended consequences.

The three key questions in the **skills boosts** will help you to evaluate consequences.

> 1. How do I identify a consequence?
> 2. How do I show that something is a consequence?
> 3. How do I decide on the main consequence?

Get started

Here is a student's plan for an answer to the exam-style question on page 51.

Intro

Overview of the circumstances leading William to undertake the Harrying of the North.

Paragraph 1

Harrying of the North: after serious 1069 rebellion when Edgar had Danish support; plus rebellion often focused on north; also northern rebellion often → rebellions elsewhere in England. Rebels didn't fight in open battle so William used same tactics as in south in 1066.

Paragraph 2

Up to 100,000 people died – killed, starved, frozen to death; homes burned, crops destroyed, reports of cannibalism; people going into slavery for food; refugee crisis – thousands fled.

Paragraph 3

William realised north of England different from south and harder to govern too – Danelaw. Explain Danelaw, link to Vikings. England always under threat from Viking invasions.

Harrying of the North weakened Danelaw: Hereward/Viking rebellion 1070–71 in East Anglia.

Paragraph 4

Pope and Church angry about Harrying of the North. William regretted it → money and time to Church; plus made Anglo-Saxon Waltheof Earl of Northumbria 1072 – gesture of reconciliation?

Conclusion

William regretted Harrying of the North for the rest of his life (remorse – gave money to Church; financial losses too), so more than just destruction of crops.

1 a Circle Ⓐ where the student has identified consequences of the Harrying of the North.

   b Cross out anything irrelevant to the question.

2 Draw an arrow on the value continuum below to show how well this plan focuses on consequence.

| Throughout (4/4 – all paragraphs) | Strongly (3/4 paragraphs) | Partially (2/4 paragraphs) | Poorly (1/4 paragraphs) | Not at all (0/4 paragraphs) |

Unit 6 Evaluating consequence

Remember this?

The Harrying of the North

This unit uses the theme of the Harrying of the North to help you build your skills in evaluating consequence. If you need to review your knowledge of this theme, work through these pages.

1 Write ✎ the dates of the following events, selecting from the choices given below.

  a Edwin and Morcar's rebellion: ....
  b The Harrying of the North: ....
  c Hereward the Wake's rebellion: ....
  d The Battle of Hastings: ....
  e Edgar Aethling and the Vikings attack York: ....

| 1066 | 1068 | 1069 | 1069–70 | 1070–71 |

2 Draw ✎ lines linking the terms below to their definitions.

terms

- A Anglo-Dane
- B Danelaw
- C Genocide
- D Guerrilla war
- E Harry
- F Waste

definition

- a Deliberate, organised attempt to wipe out an entire group of people
- b No economic activity that could be taxed
- c Where Viking power had been strongest and was still influential
- d Of mixed Anglo-Saxon and Viking ancestry
- e Devastate
- f Small bands attack larger forces by surprise then melt back into the general population

3 Circle Ⓐ how much of Yorkshire was still classed as waste in 1086.

  A 30%   B 40%
  C 50%   D 60%

4 Circle Ⓐ which of the following problems were consequences of the Harrying of the North.

  A Starvation   B Homelessness
  C Succession crisis D Refugee crisis

5 Circle Ⓐ whose death in 1069 William wanted to avenge.

  A Hugh d'Avranches   B Robert Cumin
  C Roger de Gael   D Odo of Bayeux Montgomery

6 Circle Ⓐ which years the Danes invaded England during William's reign.

  A 1068   B 1069
  C 1070   D 1075

Unit 6 Evaluating consequence

7 Tick ✓ whether the following are true or false.

		true	false
a	William also caused devastation across Wessex.	☐	☐
b	William realised the Danish threat was minor after the Harrying of the North.	☐	☐
c	The Harrying of the North was not brutal by the standards of the day.	☐	☐
d	While there were rebellions in the North, the rest of England put up no resistance to Norman rule.	☐	☐
e	Several hundred Normans were killed in York in 1069.	☐	☐
f	William saw the Harrying of the North as a great achievement.	☐	☐

8 The following statements are incorrect. Write ✎ the correct version underneath each one.

a Yorkshire was still classed as waste when the Domesday Book was compiled.

....

b The Harrying of the North was the last example of Anglo-Saxon resistance.

....

c There were between 8,000 and 15,000 fewer people in Yorkshire in 1086 than there were in 1066.

....

d William wanted to punish rebels in the North rather than meet them in open battle.

....

e The area laid waste by William stretched from the River Humber to the River Tyne.

....

9 Circle Ⓐ the odd one out and write ✎ why it is the odd one out.

a Wessex   Herefordshire   Northumbria   Staffordshire

....
....

b starvation   cannibalism   slavery   excommunication

....
....

c 1067   1068   1069   1070

....
....

54   **Unit 6 Evaluating consequence**

Skills boost

1 How do I identify a consequence?

A consequence is the result of an action or an event. Identifying consequences requires looking at the impact of events. Make sure that in an answer about consequences, your focus stays on consequences. This skills boost will help you to understand how to identify consequences.

It is essential to be able to differentiate between causes and consequences.

1 a Tick ✓ which of the following are causes that answer the question: Why did William lay waste to the North?

b Tick ✓ which of the following are consequences that answer the question: What did laying waste to the North lead to?

		question a (why?)	question b (consequence)
A	The threat of a Danish invasion of England was very serious.	☐	☐
B	After the Harrying, the Vikings raided East Anglia, as Northumbria was no longer suitable.	☐	☐
C	William wanted revenge for the slaughter of Robert Cumin.	☐	☐
D	Twenty years later, 60 per cent of Yorkshire was still classed as waste due to the Harrying.	☐	☐
E	The Harrying led to a refugee crisis as thousands fled the North.	☐	☐
F	The Harrying resulted in widespread starvation.	☐	☐
G	William wanted to put a stop to rebellion in the North.	☐	☐
H	As a result of the Harrying, the Danelaw was greatly weakened.	☐	☐
I	The impact of the Harrying on William led him to give a lot of money and time to the Church.	☐	☐
J	William needed to use different tactics to crush Anglo-Saxon resistance in the North.	☐	☐

An introduction needs to give details of consequences. It should include the one in the question and other significant ones. This is the introduction to a student's answer to the exam-style question on page 51:

> *The Harrying of the North led to Yorkshire being laid to waste, disrupting farming, which in turn led to starvation and refugees fleeing the region. It had the desired effect of putting a stop to rebellion in the North. This had been one of William's aims. Rebellion in the North often led to rebellions elsewhere. It was also a problem as the Danelaw led to close links with Vikings. As well as the deaths of up to 100,000 people, the Harrying destroyed farmland and related economic activities as long afterwards as 1086, resulting in falling revenues from the North.*

2 a Underline (A) where the consequences of the Harrying on farming have been indicated.

b Circle (A) where the student has suggested other consequences of the Harrying.

c Refer back to your list in question **1 b**. What consequences would you expect to find in the essay that are missing from the student's introduction? ✏️ ....

....

Unit 6 Evaluating consequence

Skills boost

2 How do I show that something is a consequence?

Something which happens after an event does not automatically make it a consequence of that event. For it to be a consequence, it needs to happen **as a result** of the event, or be **an effect** of it. This skills boost will demonstrate how to show that something is a consequence.

(1) All the events in the list below happened after the Harrying of the North began, but which are linked to it? Place a cross (X) alongside any that are **not** consequences of the Harrying of the North.

- A No economic activity in 60 per cent of Yorkshire, according to the Domesday Book 1086
- B William died in 1087
- C The Normanisation of the Church in 1070
- D William imprisoned Odo in 1082
- E Earls' Rebellion 1075
- F Anglo-Saxon resistance to William ended by 1071
- G No further Viking invasions of northern England
- H Thousands were slaughtered; crops, homes, livestock and seeds were destroyed

The Harrying of the North ended in 1070. It was one of many factors that made William secure on the throne until his death; however, this was **not** a direct consequence.

> There are immediate consequences and wider ones that stretch into the long term. An event can lead to a lot of different consequences, some of which link together to lead to an outcome much later on – one thing leads to another. These are called **knock-on effects**.

(2) Write down which **three** events from the list above, in which order, link the Harrying to William remaining secure on the throne until his death.

Harrying of the North ▷ ▢ ▷ ▢ ▷ ▢ ▷ William secure on throne until his death

Consequences can also be intended (planned) and unintended (unplanned) when an action is taken. They can also be positive or negative.

(3) Look at the consequences of the Harrying in the table below. Tick ✓ if they were long- or short-term, intended or unintended consequences.

Consequence	Immediate (short-term)	Long-term	Intended	Unintended
A William regretted the Harrying for the rest of his life				
B Thousands starved and froze to death				
C End to rebellion focused on the North				

56 Unit 6 Evaluating consequence

Skills boost

3 How do I decide on the main consequence?

Events usually have many different consequences. This skills boost will help you to decide which is the most important.

In order to decide what the main consequences of an event were, you need to consider its long-term consequences. You need to ask 'What did it lead to?'

1 Using the letters of the statements below, make a chain of consequences that connects the Harrying of the North to William being secure on the throne until his death.

Harrying of the North → ▢ → ▢ → ▢ → ▢ → William secure on throne until his death

A	60 per cent of Yorkshire was still 'waste' by 1086
C	There were no more Viking raids on Northumbria
E	As many as 100,000 people died

B	Danelaw was greatly weakened
D	There were no more Anglo-Saxon rebellions in northern England
F	Thousands of refugees fled the North

2 Of all the consequences A–F above, which do you think was the most important to Norman England, and why?

> You might like to consider the following when thinking about the significance of its impact:
> - Quantity: How many people were affected? How widespread was it, socially and geographically?
> - Quality: How deeply was it felt by people at the time?

....

....

....

....

....

The table below lists the consequences of William's most famous actions.

1066 Battle of Hastings	1069–70 Harrying of the North
A Large parts of south-east England immediately transferred to the Normans B Began the introduction of the feudal system C A programme of castle building was started in strategic locations	A William began replacing Anglo-Saxon aristocracy with Normans B Widely criticised, especially by the pope, and William regretted it for the rest of his life C Ended rebellion in northern England

3 Put ✏ each consequence from the lists above in the appropriate cell in the table below.

Consequence	1066	1069–70
Positive		
Negative		
Short-term		
Long-term		

Unit 6 Evaluating consequence

Sample response

Knowing what a good answer looks like can help you to model your own responses.

> **Exam-style question**
>
> 'The main consequence of the Harrying of the North was the destruction of crops and farming land.'
>
> How far do you agree? Explain your answer.
>
> You may use the following in your answer:
> - wasteland
> - Vikings
>
> You **must** also use information of your own. (16 marks)

Read the following student's answer to the exam-style question above.

> The Harrying of the North had very important consequences for William. It is said that he regretted it for the rest of his life. It resulted in there being no more rebellions in the north of England. This was possibly the most important consequence for William, as rebellions there triggered them elsewhere, stretching his resources. So for him it was a very positive outcome and to this extent he achieved his aim. However, there was the unintended and very negative consequence of the pope's criticism and William spending a lot of time and money making amends.
>
> Perhaps the most shocking consequence was the death of up to 100,000 people. Some historians say it was genocide.
>
> The Harrying led to the immediate consequence of the destruction of farming, with the knock-on effect of thousands starving to death over the next year or so. As farming was the main economic activity and source of income, its devastation had serious knock-on, long-term impacts on almost all parts of the North's economy too. In 1086, the Domesday Book recorded that 60 per cent of Yorkshire was still waste. This would not have been what William intended, as his revenues suffered in the long run as a consequence. It was certainly a negative consequence for him and far worse for the people of the North.

(1) Look for the following strengths:

  a Draw ✏ an asterisk (*) where the stated consequence in the question has been directly addressed.

  b Circle Ⓐ where consequences other than the one stated in the question are identified.

  c Underline Ⓐ where the type of consequence is referenced (e.g. intended/unintended).

  d Double underline Ⓐ where the importance of the consequences is mentioned.

58   Unit 6 Evaluating consequence

Your turn!

Get back on track

Now it's your turn to try to answer an exam-style question.

Exam-style question

'The main consequence of the Harrying of the North was the reduction in Crown revenues.'

How far do you agree? Explain your answer.

You may use the following in your answer:
- wasteland
- Vikings

You **must** also use information of your own.

(16 marks)

1. Write ✎ two paragraphs in the space below focusing on the consequences of the Harrying of the North. Identify the types of consequences you write about. Here is a list of different types of consequences for you to think about:

| Immediate | Long-term | Knock-on | Unintended | Positive | Negative |

2. At the end of the second paragraph, using terms from the list in ① to justify your argument, say whether you think the most important consequence of the Harrying of the North was the reduction in Crown revenues. ✎

Unit 6 Evaluating consequence 59

Review your skills

Check up

Review your response to the exam-style question on page 59. Tick ✓ the column to show how well you think you have done each of the following.

	Had a go ✓	Nearly there ✓	Got it! ✓
clearly identified key consequences	☐	☐	☐
focused on consequences	☐	☐	☐
made judgements about how significant the consequences were	☐	☐	☐
supported judgements about consequences	☐	☐	☐

Look over all of your work in this unit. Note down three things you have learned that you will apply when evaluating consequence.

1 ....
2 ....
3 ....

Need more practice?

On separate paper, plan and write your response to the exam-style question below.

> **Exam-style question**
>
> 'The main consequence of William creating new earldoms after Hastings was Anglo-Saxon rebellions.'
>
> How far do you agree? Explain your answer.
>
> You may use the following in your answer:
> - Edwin and Morcar
> - Marcher earldoms
>
> You **must** also use information of your own.
>
> (16 marks)

How confident do you feel about each of these **skills**? Colour in the bars.

1. How do I identify a consequence?
2. How do I show that something is a consequence?
3. How do I decide on the main consequence?

Unit 6 Evaluating consequence

Get started

7 Making judgements

There is no such thing as a 'right' judgement; there is such a thing as a 'good' or convincing judgement. There is a challenge in doing this: you cannot ignore important evidence because it doesn't fit your answer! This unit will help you to develop the skills to make judgements effectively. The skills you will build are how to:

- organise information to make a judgement
- deal with conflicting evidence
- make a convincing judgement.

In the exam, you will be asked to tackle questions such as the one below. This unit will prepare you to write your own response to this type of question.

> **Exam-style question**
>
> 'The main reason for the submission of the earls in 1066 was fear of William.'
>
> How far do you agree? Explain your answer.
>
> You may use the following in your answer:
>
> - Berkhamsted
> - the Battle of Hastings
>
> You **must** also use information of your own. (16 marks)

The signs of strong judgements in an essay include:

- the judgement is in the introduction and can be followed through to the conclusion
- the relative importance of the stated factor compared with other factors is considered
- evidence that doesn't fit the judgement is dealt with
- the focus on the question is maintained and the answer links back to it throughout.

Here are some more points to remember about making judgements:

- For 'how far do you agree' questions, your judgement will be how far you agree!
- Judgements on historical questions are unlikely to be 100% agreement or disagreement; be prepared to challenge the statement!

You will need to apply your skills from Unit 5, on evaluating significance, to help you reach your judgements.

The three key questions in the **skills boosts** will help you to answer judgement questions effectively.

1. How do I use my information to make a judgement?
2. How do I deal with conflicting evidence?
3. How do I ensure I make a convincing judgement?

Unit 7 Making judgements 61

Get started

A student planning an answer to the exam-style question on page 61 gathered the following evidence.

> 1. Edgar Aethling had been considered too young to be king after Edward died.
> 2. William had brutally destroyed swathes of the south-east after the Battle of Hastings.
> 3. Edgar Aethling had only recently arrived in England, without any 'ready-made' support.
> 4. Anglo-Saxon bishops and archbishops were to keep their positions.
> 5. William's position was strong: he had secured the south and supply routes to Normandy.
> 6. William promised that Edwin could marry his daughter, which could have made him very powerful in the new, Norman kingdom.
> 7. The earls held London, which was fortified, but William's army was threatening to cut it off.
> 8. The earls kept much of their land: Mercia (Edwin) and Northumbria (Morcar).

First, he counted how many pieces of evidence supported the idea that fear of William was the most important factor in bringing about the submission of the earls.

1 a How many pieces of evidence in the list above directly suggest that fear of William caused the earls' submission? ....

   b Based on your answer to **1 a**, how important was it as a reason for their submission? Tick your choice.

A	Very important – 5 or more pieces of evidence	☐
B	Quite important – 3–4 pieces of evidence	☐
C	Not very important – 1–2 pieces of evidence	☐

   c Repeat **1 a** and **b** for the other possible reasons for the earls' submission suggested below.

   A | Submission was an act of self-interest on the part of the Anglo-Saxon earls.

   ....

   B | The submission of the earls happened because the earls' position was weak.

   ....

   C | The submission of the earls came about because Edgar Aethling was not a credible alternative to rally around.

   ....

2 Review your answers to **1**. According to the quantities of evidence, which was/were the most important reason(s) for the earls' submission?

....

....

3 What drawbacks are there in using this method (counting up the pieces of evidence) to come to a judgement?

....

....

Unit 7 Making judgements

Remember this?

The Battle of Hastings and its aftermath

This unit uses the theme of what happened after the Battle of Hastings to build your skills in making judgements. If you need to review your knowledge of this theme, work through these pages.

1 Circle Ⓐ which of the following were problems faced by Harold at Hastings.

- A | Not all the fyrd levies turned up
- B | Too few archers
- C | A much smaller army than William's
- D | Shield wall collapsing

2 Circle Ⓐ which of the following were strategies used by William at Hastings.

- A | Sending in foot soldiers last
- B | Cavalry charges
- C | Sending in foot soldiers first
- D | Cutting off some of Harold's army

3 Circle Ⓐ which of the following were features of housecarls.

- A | Fought with maces
- B | Fought on foot
- C | Fought with axes
- D | Carried round shields

4 Circle Ⓐ which of the following were features of William's knights.

- A | They could stand up in the saddle to fight
- B | They carried round shields
- C | They carried kite-shaped shields
- D | Specially bred and trained horses

5 Tick ✓ to show whether the statements below are true or false.   true   false

- a | The weakening of William's shield wall was a turning point in the Battle of Hastings.
- b | William made sure his soldiers treated the people around Hastings with great respect.
- c | William brought a castle with him from Normandy.
- d | After the Battle of Hastings, William made Odo of Bayeux Archbishop of Canterbury.
- e | After the Battle of Hastings, William marched straight to London to force the Anglo-Saxon earls to surrender.
- f | William offered Edwin his daughter's hand in marriage.

Unit 7 Making judgements

Remember this?

6 Circle Ⓐ what happened to the survivors of Harold's army after Hastings.

- A | They were taken hostage
- B | They were executed
- C | They fled to London
- D | They formally surrendered

7 Circle Ⓐ where the Anglo-Saxons had the best chance of defeating William after Hastings.

- A | Dover
- B | Canterbury
- C | London
- D | Berkhamsted

8 Circle Ⓐ the reason why there was an opportunity to defeat William after Hastings.

- A | He and his men ran out of supplies
- B | The people of Kent rebelled against him
- C | Edgar arrived with a fresh army
- D | William and his men fell ill

9 Circle Ⓐ where the Anglo-Saxon earls finally submitted to William.

- A | Winchester
- B | London
- C | Berkhamsted
- D | Wallingford

10
a. Why was it important that William captured Winchester?
....

b. When was William's coronation?
....

c. What right did William say those who fought against him at Hastings had lost?
....

11 The following statements are incorrect. Write ✏ the correct version underneath each one.

a. | After Hastings, William gave Edwin and Morcar's lands to Odo and FitzOsbern.
....

b. | William met with Edwin and Morcar at Wallingford to negotiate the terms of their submission.
....

c. | William's brutal strategy in the south of England led to resistance from the towns on his way to London.
....

d. | Gospatric was made Earl of Northumbria after paying William a large sum of money.
....

Unit 7 Making judgements

Skills boost

1. How do I use my information to make a judgement?

When using the information you have to make a judgement, do not simply look at the quantity of evidence you have for any one cause, consequence or change. This skills boost will help you to consider the impact of evidence you have on the outcome you are studying.

1 Use the evidence from page 62 to complete the table below.

Evidence suggesting fear of William was important	Evidence linking fear of William to other causes	Evidence suggesting fear of William was not important

Don't just look at the **quantity** of evidence. Think about how different events and circumstances would **contribute** to the outcome. Some would play a very important role, others a lesser one.

2 Taking all the evidence into consideration, draw an arrow on the continuum below what you think about whether fear of William was the most important reason for the submission of the earls in 1066. Briefly explain your choice below.

Disagree 100%	Disagree strongly	Disagree more than agree	Agree more than disagree	Agree strongly	Agree 100%

3 The student from page 62 decided the weakness of the earls' position was the most important reason for the submission of the earls in 1066. Which of these plans is better for answering the question? Explain your choice using the guidelines given in the Introduction to this unit.

> Use your skills on evaluation of significance from Unit 5 to help you make your judgement.

Plan A
1. Explain why the earls' weak position was the most important reason.
2. Explain why the earls' self-interest is next most important; + links to earls' weak position.
3. Explain why Edgar Aethling not being credible was less important; + links to earls' weak position.
4. Explain why I disagree fear of William was very important; + links to earls' weak position.

Plan B
1. Explain why fear of William was important but not the **most** important reason.
2. Explain why earls' weak position was most important reason; + links to fear of William.
3. Explain why self-interest was next most important reason; + links to fear of William.
4. Explain why Edgar Aethling was less important reason; + links to fear of William.

Skills boost

2. How do I deal with conflicting evidence?

Knowing how to deal with conflicting evidence is very important in making effective judgements. This skills boost will help you understand how to deal with conflicting evidence.

So, was the fear of William the most important reason for the earls' submission in 1066?

A Yes, fear of William was the most important reason. His reputation and brutal tactics meant people were surrendering to him wherever he went. As he continued the destruction, the earls were in danger of being cut off in London, so they submitted.

B The Anglo-Saxon earls weren't afraid. The Witan was ready to carry on with Edgar as king and they occupied London. There it became clear he wasn't credible. Edgar and the earls couldn't agree on a plan, and without Winchester there wasn't the means to raise an army.

C It all came down to self-interest. They submitted in return for William promising to be a 'good and gracious' lord. He promised Edwin his daughter, they got back a lot of their land in the North, and Anglo-Saxons kept important Church posts.

D The earls wanted to carry on but their position was too weak. They didn't need Edgar, but once William had the Treasury they couldn't raise another army. Nor could they agree on a plan. With London's supplies in danger of being cut off, they submitted.

Conflicting evidence can help to establish a debate in your answer, either by looking more carefully at why it conflicts, or by acknowledging the differences. You could use the following phrases in your answer.

> **Why is there conflicting evidence? Because it can vary according to when, who, where**
> - While X was more important when …, Y became more important when … (time frame)
> - Although X was more important to …, Y was more important to … (different people/groups)
> - Although X was more important where …, Y was more important where … (geography)
>
> **Acknowledge the differences**
> - It is true that X was at least partly a reason for … However, Y cannot be ignored because …
> - Although X was certainly a factor in …, Y was perhaps more important because …
> - From one point of view, X can be seen as more important because …, but from another, Y is …

Read the statements A–D.

1 a Why is there conflict between A and B? ....

....

   b Why is there conflict between C and D? ....

....

2 Using the phrases in the box, write a sentence combining the conflicting evidence in

   a B and D. ....

....

   b A and C. ....

....

66 **Unit 7 Making judgements**

Skills boost

3 How do I ensure I make a convincing judgement?

A convincing judgement is the one you most believe in after weighing the evidence and taking other options into account. This skills boost will help you to make a convincing judgement.

A student made the following notes for an answer to this question:

Exam-style question

'The most important reason for the submission of the earls in 1066 was self-interest.'

How far do you agree? Explain your answer.

A convincing judgement will:
- focus on the question – use the key words from the question to start your judgement
- weigh up *all* the evidence – acknowledge that there are alternative points of view
- support your judgement – identify and explain the key evidence that led to your judgement.

> Self-interest → submission of the earls: Edwin to marry William's daughter; earls kept much of their land: Mercia (Edwin), Northumbria (Morcar); Anglo-Saxons continued to hold all top Church positions; William promising to be a 'good and gracious' lord to the Anglo-Saxons.
>
> Earls' position weak: William held the south coast of England; his brutal progress → southern towns quickly surrendering; earls in London; William in danger of cutting them off from supplies and reinforcements from the north; Edgar not effective, couldn't agree with earls on what to do.

To answer the exam-style question at the top of the page, one student's judgement using the notes above was that it was largely self-interest that led the earls to submit.

(1) Underline (A) the evidence in the student's notes above that best supports their judgement. Look back at page 65 if you need some help.

Two students' judgements were that it was weakness of the earls' position that led them to submit to William. One gave Edgar not being an effective king as the strongest evidence for this; the other gave William's brutal progress through the south of England.

(2) Which student's choice of supporting evidence makes a stronger, more convincing point? Explain your choice, remembering to weigh the evidence and consider all options. Your choice will be the one that you believe in and can explain persuasively.

Remember: The question is **how far** self-interest was the most important reason for the submission of the earls in 1066.

Unit 7 Making judgements

Sample response

Get back on track

Making effective judgements is an important skill. Knowing the difference between a convincing and an unconvincing judgement will help you to model your own.

> **Exam-style question**
>
> 'The main reason for the submission of the earls in 1066 was fear of William.'
>
> How far do you agree? Explain your answer.

In response to the exam-style question above, a student wrote the judgement below.

> Fear of William was an important factor in the submission of the earls in 1066. By the time he had reached Berkhamsted, William had destroyed south-east England. From one point of view fear of William can be seen as important because of its impact on southern England; from another it was the earls' self-interest that was. Events in southern England suggested that the earls were likely to lose and could expect harsh treatment from William.
>
> More important, however, was the weakness of the earls' position. Fear of William led towns to surrender to him and reinforced this weakness, especially as William had taken Winchester, and so the Treasury. This meant that there was no way to pay for another army even if one could be raised. Edgar, although elected king by the Witan, had only recently returned to England and had no army of his own. He took no decisive action against William, suggesting either a lack of experience or that he and the earls could not agree about what to do. Although it is true that the weakness of the earls' position was most important to their submission, it is also true that Edgar's lack of credibility was at least partly a reason for that. Likewise, while the earls' own self-interest was partly a factor, the weakness of their position was more important because by the time they submitted it was so bad that there was little real alternative.

The judgement shows the following strengths:

- It deals with the stated factor, despite not believing it was the most important cause. This means it has directly addressed the question.
- It gives a clear judgement about what the most important cause is.
- It shows the relative importance of the key causes compared with its most important cause. This means it has not ignored the evidence that doesn't fit with its judgement.
- It provides support for its judgement. This means that it shows the reasoning behind the judgement.

1
  a   Highlight where a judgement on the importance of the stated factor (fear of William) as a cause has been made.

  b   Underline where a judgement about the most important cause has been made.

  c   Circle any evidence or reasons put forward to support the weakness of the earls' position as the most important cause of their submission.

  d   Draw an asterisk (*) where words and phrases have addressed conflicting evidence.

  e   Pick one sentence you think best presents the student's point of view and double underline it. Look for a clearly explained, well-supported point that summarises their view as to why the earls submitted.

Your turn!

Get back on track

Now it's your turn to try to answer an exam-style question.

Exam-style question

'Self-interest was the most important reason for the submission of the earls in 1066.'

How far do you agree? Explain your answer.

You may use the following in your answer:

- Berkhamsted
- the Battle of Hastings

You **must** also use information of your own.

(16 marks)

1. What evidence is there that self-interest was the most important reason for the submission of the earls? On a separate piece of paper, draw up this table to help you decide.

Evidence yes	Evidence no

2. From your 'Evidence no' column, what reasons other than self-interest are there?

....

....

3. Write 2–3 sentences supporting the view in the question.

....

....

4. Write 2–3 sentences supporting another reason (your choice) for the earls' submission.

....

....

5. Bring your answers to 3 and 4 together in a short paragraph that explains which reason is the most important and to what extent. It should also include the other, conflicting point of view – to what extent was it important in comparison?

....

....

....

....

....

....

....

Unit 7 Making judgements

Review your skills

Check up

Review your response to the exam-style question on page 69. Tick ✓ the column to show how well you think you have done each of the following.

	Had a go ✓	Nearly there ✓	Got it! ✓
used my information to develop an effective judgement	☐	☐	☐
considered deciding factors to assess how far I agree with the statement	☐	☐	☐
looked at the stated feature in comparison with other causes	☐	☐	☐
dealt with conflicting evidence in making my judgement	☐	☐	☐

Look over all of your work in this unit. Note down three things you have learned that you will apply when making judgements.

1. ....
2. ....
3. ....

Need more practice?

On separate paper, plan and write your response to the exam-style question below.

Exam-style question

'The most important reason for Edwin and Morcar's rebellion of 1068 was their resentment over loss of lands.'

How far do you agree? Explain your answer.

You may use the following in your answer:
- changes to land ownership
- the geld tax

You **must** also use information of your own.

(16 marks)

How confident do you feel about each of these **skills**? Colour in the bars.

1. How do I use my information to make a judgement?
2. How do I deal with conflicting evidence?
3. How do I ensure I make a convincing judgement?

Get started

8 Writing effective conclusions

This unit will help you to develop the skills to write conclusions effectively. The skills you will build are how to:

- recognise the features of a successful conclusion
- show in the conclusion why one element is more important than others
- construct an effective conclusion.

In the exam, you will be asked to tackle questions such as the one below. This unit will prepare you to write your own response to this type of question.

> **Exam-style question**
>
> 'The main reason why William was able to centralise power was because he increased the royal demesne.'
>
> How far do you agree? Explain your answer.
>
> You may use the following in your answer:
>
> - the Domesday Book
> - the forest
>
> You **must** also include information of your own. (16 marks)

Effective conclusions should:

- answer the question directly
- reinforce the judgement made in the essay (without using any new material)
- show why you have chosen a cause/consequence/change/feature over others in the essay
- have a final sentence that links back to the question.

The three key questions in the **skills boosts** will help you to write conclusions effectively.

1. What are the features of an effective conclusion?
2. How do I show why one element is more important than others?
3. How do I construct an effective conclusion?

Unit 8 Writing effective conclusions   71

Get started

One important feature of an effective conclusion is that it does **not** contain any new information.

Students had the following information available to them to use in answering the exam-style question on page 71.

A William increased royal demesne so that he was the biggest landholder. He would also be the wealthiest.	**B** Norman sheriffs were the undisputed leaders of their shires and answerable only to William.	**C** Thegns were destroyed as a class as they became the vassals of Norman tenants-in-chief.
D Under the feudal system, all knights owed their loyalty to William, not the tenants-in-chief.	**E** William used grants and forfeits to ensure loyalty and to reduce the size and powers of the earldoms.	**F** William added new laws to punish rebellion against Norman control, which the sheriffs enforced.

1 a Amy used evidence A, C, D and E in her essay and summarised it in her conclusion. Which of the three conclusions below did she write? ....

b Sanjay used evidence B, D and F in his essay and summarised it in his conclusion. Which of the three conclusions below did he write? ....

Conclusion 1
> The most important reason that William could centralise power was the sheriffs. They enforced his new laws against rebellion, were the undisputed leaders of their shires and answered only to William. This gave William control over more land than just the royal demesne. It also reduced the power of tenants-in-chief, whose knights owed their loyalty directly to the king.

Conclusion 2
> Changes in landholding were the most important reason why William was able to centralise power. Part of this was increasing the royal demesne, which he did by using grants and forfeits to keep his vassals in line. The Normanisation of the Church was also important. The land it held, one quarter of England, was no longer in Anglo-Saxon hands after 1070.

Conclusion 3
> The feudal system enabled William's centralisation of power. Since he was king, even the tenants-in-chief were answerable to him, and he used grants and forfeits of land to keep them loyal. Even their knights owed direct loyalty to the king. Furthermore, thegns were replaced by knights. These changes gave William more control than increasing royal demesne.

2 Label Amy's and Sanjay's conclusions with the relevant letters A–F to show where their sentences have used the evidence from those cards.

3 Which conclusion do you think answers the question the most fully? Explain your answer.

> **Remember:** A conclusion should not introduce new points; it should reinforce points you have already made.

Conclusion .... because ....

....

....

....

....

Unit 8 Writing effective conclusions

Remember this?

Norman government

This unit uses the theme of Norman government to build your skills in writing effective conclusions. If you need to review your knowledge of this theme, work through these pages.

1 Draw lines linking each term to its definition.

term	description
A Royal demesne	a Land kept by the king for hunting, with harsher laws
B Fief	b Public demonstration of allegiance to another person
C Homage	c Ruled England on William's behalf when he was in Normandy
D Tenants-in-chief	d Land kept by the king for his own use
E Regents	e Held land directly from the king
F Forest	f Land held by a vassal in return for service to a lord
G Centralise	g Person in charge of a castle
H Castellan	h Concentrate control under a single authority

2 Fill in the gaps with the words listed below. There are more words than gaps.

William introduced payments called .... that landholders' .... made to reclaim their inheritance. The amount was decided by .... , and he rewarded .... by agreeing small amounts. He could also use .... of land to punish disobedient .... During his reign, William decreased the size of .... and increased the .... Fines for breaking the harsh .... laws were a very good source of .... for William.

| earldoms | forest | forfeits | geld | heirs | income | loyalty | reliefs |
| royal council | royal demesne | sheriffs' | tax | thegns | vassals | William |

3 What did the Domesday Book record?

....
....
....

Unit 8 Writing effective conclusions 73

Remember this?

4 In each of the groups below, circle Ⓐ the odd one out and say why it is the odd one out.

  a | homage | relief | geld | fines |
  ....

  b | under-tenants | tenants-in-chief | slaves | peasants |
  ....

  c | bishops | regents | knights | sheriffs |
  ....

  d | Church | manor | baronial | regent |
  ....

5 Circle Ⓐ which of the following the Domesday Book survey was concerned with.

  A | Landowners' heirs | B | Who owned what land |
  C | Who owed what tax | D | Who controlled water sources |

6 Circle Ⓐ which of the following were forbidden in the forest.

  A | Clearing trees | B | Poaching |
  C | Carrying hunting weapons | D | Constructing buildings |

7 Circle Ⓐ which of the following were rights that sheriffs had.

  A | Hunting in the forest | B | Answerable to no one but the king |
  C | Introducing their own taxes in the shire | D | Keeping a share of revenues collected |

8 Circle Ⓐ what things peasants owed for their land.

  A | Labour service | B | Some of the produce |
  C | Rents | D | Military service |

9 The statements below are incorrect. Write ✎ the correct version under each one.

  a | Those who killed deer in the royal forest were beheaded. |
  ....

  b | William introduced the geld tax from Normandy. |
  ....

  c | Sheriffs were also castellans. |
  ....

  d | New bishops did homage to the pope. |
  ....

74 **Unit 8 Writing effective conclusions**

Skills boost

1 What are the features of an effective conclusion?

A conclusion must: answer the question directly, reinforce the judgement in the essay and show why you have chosen one element over another. This skills boost will help you to recognise these features.

Exam-style question

'The main reason why William was able to centralise power was because he increased the royal demesne.'

How far do you agree? Explain your answer.

A student answering the question above decided that the feudal system was the main reason why William was able to centralise power. They wrote the following conclusion.

> Although increasing the royal demesne was quite significant in William centralising power, because he increased his own landholding, revenues and therefore power, the feudal system and sheriffs were more important. Sheriffs, as the undisputed leaders of the shires answerable only to the king, helped William to strengthen his grip on power more directly. The feudal system was most important because, as its head, William used grants and forfeits to directly control potentially powerful earls. Powerful earls could undermine the king. Overall, the feudal system was much more important than increasing the royal demesne in William centralising power, because it was the feudal system that gave him control over those most likely to be a challenge to him.

Remember: You need to show why you have chosen one cause/consequence/change/feature over others in answering your question. This reasoning will inform the judgement you present in your conclusion.

1.
   a. Highlight where the stated factor has been dealt with.
   b. Circle where the most important reason why William was able to centralise power is given.
   c. Underline the reasoning that shows why the most important cause/consequence/change/feature is used.
   d. Double underline where the question is answered directly.

Another student decided that reducing the size of earldoms was the most important reason.

2.
   a. Circle the statement that gives the judgement about the most important reason why William was able to centralise power.
   b. Highlight the phrases that explain why the student chose that reason over the others.

   A | Increasing the royal demesne was simply another way of reducing the size of the earldoms and so was less important to centralising power.

   B | Reducing the size of earldoms was much more important to William centralising power than increasing the royal demesne.

   C | Reducing the size of the earldoms was more important because it enabled William to control the earls better, and the earls to control their lands more effectively.

Unit 8 Writing effective conclusions

Skills boost

2 How do I show why one element is more important than others?

You will need to show your reasoning for choosing one cause/consequence/change/feature over any others in answering your question. This skills boost will help you to show in your conclusion why you consider one element to be more important than others.

Exam-style question

'Sheriffs were the main reason William was able to centralise power.'

How far do you agree? Explain your answer.

(1) Which of the statements A–H below link with the following three reasons why William was able to centralise power? (Some statements might link with more than one reason.)

  a Sheriffs were the main reason: ....
  b Normanisation of the Church was the main reason: ....
  c Feudal system was the main reason: ....

A	William used grants and forfeits of land to control earls and stop them becoming too powerful.	B	The Norman Church made sure the people received positive messages about William and the Normans.	C	Under the feudal system, knights had to swear allegiance to William, not their tenants-in-chief.
D	Sheriffs were the undisputed leaders of their shire, answerable only to William.	E	The king oversaw Church councils and his approval was needed for key decisions.	F	New bishops did homage to the king. William could use forfeits against the clergy too.
G	Sheriffs enforced laws, including punishing rebellion against Norman control.			H	By 1087 there were only two Anglo-Saxon tenants-in-chief. Most thegns had Norman lords.

(2) Which of the three reasons do you think had the biggest impact on William being able to centralise power?

....

(3) Look at your answer to (2). If you had to pick one statement from A–H above to justify your decision, which would it be and why?

  I would choose .... because ....
  ....

(4) On a separate piece of paper, write your conclusion to answer the exam-style question above. Use this checklist as a guide.

> The conclusion does not cover every reason for your judgement; that is done in the essay. Your conclusion uses reasoning to reinforce what led you to choose one element over the others.

Checklist	✓
Answer the question directly. How far was the stated factor the main reason?	
Identify the most important factor.	
Explain why you have chosen one factor over the others.	
Make sure your final sentence links back to the question.	

Unit 8 Writing effective conclusions

Skills boost

3 How do I construct an effective conclusion?

An effective conclusion should clearly reinforce your arguments and prove to the reader how convincing they are. This skills boost will help you to structure the features of a successful conclusion.

A | This was more important than increasing the royal demesne because reducing and redistributing earls' powers gave William more actual power.

B | Although increasing royal demesne was important, his handling of tenants-in-chief had more direct impact on centralising power.

C | Two other important contributing factors were Normanising the Church (bishops were reliant upon him for their lands and status) and making sheriffs the undisputed leaders in the shires, answerable only to the king.

D | The most important factor in William centralising power was reducing the power of tenants-in-chief.

E | So reducing William's handling of the tenants-in-chief was the most important reason why he centralised power.

F | For example, reducing the size of earldoms and using grants and forfeits to ensure loyalty kept potential rivals in line, reinforcing William's own power.

(1) Sentences **A–F** above are taken from a strong conclusion asking students how far they agree with the statement: 'Increasing the royal demesne was the main reason William was able to centralise power.' The conclusion has all the characteristics listed in the table below. Match the sentences with the characteristics listed in the table by writing ✎ the letters **A–F** in the right-hand column.

Key characteristics of a strong conclusion	Which statement shows which characteristic? ✎
a Statement giving what you believe to be the most important factor	
b Statement on how far you agree with the stated factor	
c Explanation of your choice of most important element and why it is more important than any others	
d Bring in the relative importance of any other factors	
e Reinforce your conclusion about the most important factor and how it relates to the stated factor and other factors	
f Statement giving what you believe to be the most important factor	

Sample response

Knowing how to write an effective conclusion is very important in convincing the reader of the arguments you presented. Knowing the difference between an effective and ineffective conclusion will help you when it comes to writing your own.

A student using the information from page 72 wrote the following conclusion to this exam-style question:

Exam-style question

'The main reason why William was able to centralise power was the sheriffs.'

How far do you agree? Explain your answer.

> The feudal system that William imposed ensured that tenants-in-chief and their knights owed loyalty to him and this kept them within his control. Land could be granted but also forfeited, so William could directly control the fates of earls. Although earls could be sheriffs, William could also take the position away from them if he wished. William's powerful position at the top of the feudal system was reinforced by the Normanisation of the Church. Not only were bishops also tenants-in-chief (so they were part of the feudal system), but they also ensured that the people accepted William's government because he had God's approval, as Hastings had shown. The sheriffs were undisputed leaders of the shires, answerable only to the king.

(1) Which element does the student say was the most important?

(2) Underline (A) the reasoning the student uses to show why this element was so important.

(3) Other than the stated and most important elements, which other element does the conclusion mention?

(4) Why does the student think that the Normanisation of the Church was less important?

The student's conclusion could be stronger. To be effective, their paragraph needs to start by answering the question directly and giving the judgement. It also needs a final sentence linking back to the question.

(5) Write the opening 2–3 sentences of a conclusion in answer to the exam-style question above.

(6) Write a final sentence that rounds off the answer, linking back to the question.

Unit 8 Writing effective conclusions

Your turn!

Now it's your turn to try to answer an exam-style question.

> **Exam-style question**
>
> 'The main reason why William was able to strengthen his grip on power was because he Normanised the Church.'
>
> How far do you agree? Explain your answer.
>
> You may use the following in your answer:
>
> - bishops
> - the Domesday Book
>
> You **must** also use information of your own. **(16 marks)**

1 Use the information below to write a conclusion to the question. As well as the stated element, the other two to think about are **England's economy** and **increasing the royal demesne**.

A	The king oversaw Church councils and his approval was needed for key decisions.
B	Bishops were tenants-in-chief, so clergy who failed William could forfeit their land.
C	Norman bishops and archdeacons ensured people heard favourable things about the king.
D	Claiming all England enabled William to grant and take away land, giving him great power.
E	William had tight control of the forest and made a lot of extra revenue from fines.
F	William reduced the size of earldoms and the powers of the Marcher earldoms after 1071.
G	William controlled reliefs, using them to increase revenues and ensure loyalty.
H	William controlled taxation. The geld was the most important to extract England's wealth.
I	The Domesday Book ensured that William knew who held what land, taxes and services.

> Do not attempt to include all of the information above in the conclusion. Use only the information that best helps you to explain your reasoning.
> - Answer the question directly. How far was the stated element the main reason?
> - Identify the most important element.
> - Explain why you have chosen one element over the others.
> - Make sure your final sentence links back to the question.

Unit 8 Writing effective conclusions

Review your skills

Check up

Review your response to the exam-style question on page 79. Tick ✓ the column to show how well you think you have done each of the following.

	Had a go ✓	Nearly there ✓	Got it! ✓
understood the features of an effective conclusion	☐	☐	☐
shown in the conclusion how one element is more important than others	☐	☐	☐
summarised and reinforced my arguments to construct an effective conclusion	☐	☐	☐

Look over all of your work in this unit. Note down three things you have learned that you will apply when writing an effective conclusion.

1 ....
2 ....
3 ....

Need more practice?

On separate paper, plan and write your response to the exam-style question below.

Exam-style question

'The main reason why the Church was reformed in 1070 was to help William strengthen his control of England.'

How far do you agree? Explain your answer.

You may use the following in your answer:

- Lanfranc
- the Normanisation of the Church

You **must** also use information of your own.

(16 marks)

How confident do you feel about each of these **skills**? Colour in the bars.

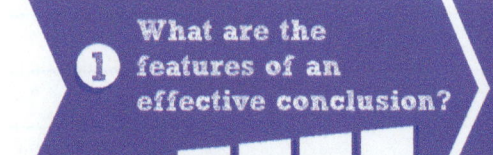

1. What are the features of an effective conclusion?
2. How do I show why one element is more important than others?
3. How do I construct an effective conclusion?

Unit 8 Writing effective conclusions

Answers

Where an example answer is given, this is not necessarily the only correct response. In most cases there is a range of responses that can gain full marks.

Unit 1

Page 2

1 **a–d**

Marcher earldoms came with more power than other earldoms because they were so important for England's defence. For example, Marcher earls did not have to apply to the king for permission to build castles. ~~Castles were vital to England's defence too, and William I built them all over England as a means of controlling the Anglo-Saxons.~~ Marcher earls also did not have to pay taxes.

Page 3

1 A = e, h
B = b, f
C = a, c
D = d, g

2
- a true
- b true
- c true
- d false
- e true
- f false
- g false
- h true

Page 4

3 Odo

4 **Anglo-Saxon:** Burh, Fyrd, Thegn, Witan
Norman: Fief, Marcher earldom
Both: Earl, Sheriff

5
- a William Rufus – the others all fought against him in the succession crisis after William I's death.
- b Winchester – the others are all Marcher earldoms.
- c Silver pennies – the others were all introduced by the Normans.

6
- a A, D
- b A, B, D
- c A, B, C, D
- d B

Page 5

1

	Key feature?	Why? (Long-term trend)	Why? (One of many such examples)
A			
B	✓		✓
C	✓	✓	
D	✓	✓	
E	✓		✓

2 William I established the feudal system in England, at the top of which were his tenants-in-chief. Odo and William FitzOsbern, both Normans, were two of the most important. Tenants-in-chief were very powerful, having their own knights and much land. Their role was to help William defend and govern England. He also appointed regents to govern England in his absence. Queen Matilda frequently took this role. Odo and FitzOsbern both acted as regents for him too. However, their poor government and land grabbing was the cause of a rebellion when they were regents for him in 1067.

Page 6

1 a

	Relevant	Specific	One of many examples
A	✓	✓	✓
B	✓	✓	✓
C	✓		
D			
E	✓	✓	
F	✓	✓	

b A and B are the strongest examples of supporting detail, having 3 ticks each.

2 One key feature of William I's government was his use of sheriffs. They were expected to control their shires and were answerable to William only, making them very powerful. ~~There was resentment against sheriffs as they were often involved in land grabs from Anglo-Saxons.~~ Another feature was that William used royal councils, ~~much like the Anglo-Saxon Witan,~~ when he needed advice or support. In 1085, for example, he called a council because there were fears of a Viking invasion.

Page 7

1 **Feature 1:** One key feature of Norman knights was that they owed the king 40 days of knight service a year, making them an important and cheap way of providing defence for the kingdom because it was their lords who had to foot the bill. The Anglo-Saxon word for knight was cniht. The word cniht/knight means 'household retainer', which means someone who follows an important person.

Feature 2: Knights had an important role in controlling England. They played a key part in law and order as they were often lords of the manor and settled disputes in their manorial courts. Tenants-in-chief also held their own courts. ~~Norman knights were elite cavalry troops, vital to William's army. They were able to charge their opponents' ranks with devastating effect, causing them to scatter.~~ Because they were on horseback, they had kite-shaped shields and their chainmail was split so that their legs were protected.

Answers 81

Page 8

1

	Strengths	Weaknesses
Feature 1	One key feature Relevant to question Supporting detail	Defines historical term (burh)
Feature 2	There is one key feature, supported by relevant detail; this will be enough to gain the 2 marks.	Gives more than one key feature (role in controlling England; knights' role as William's army) Includes unnecessary description (Anglo-Saxon earldoms were much larger) Irrelevant material (tenants-in-chief had their own courts)

Page 9

1 Student's own response.

Unit 2

Page 12

1

a There are five pieces of filler:

Lanfranc, who was known to be a reformer, replaced the Anglo-Saxon Archbishop of Canterbury, Stigand, in 1070. ~~Lanfranc was very close to William. He became so powerful he was able to crown William's favourite son king in 1087 without consulting anyone.~~ Many of Lanfranc's reforms, which are known as Normanisation, greatly strengthened William I's position. For example, under Lanfranc, William I controlled all communication with the pope in Rome. ~~The pope is the leader of the Roman Catholic Church.~~ Lanfranc's reforms made the Church much more disciplined, with greater control over parish priests, who were made to follow Norman procedures and customs. The Church was also very important in making sure the people – especially the Anglo-Saxons – heard favourable things about the king. Priests taught that God was on the Normans' side at Hastings, for example. ~~Lanfranc was very much William's man. He agreed that William must be in charge of communication between the pope and the English Church.~~ This shows that Lanfranc's reforms were helpful to William I, strengthening his position.

b Answers could include:

A = unnecessary/irrelevant background description

C = unnecessary/irrelevant description beyond scope of question

E and B repeat each other – better to get rid of B as it focuses on Anglo-Saxons

G = unnecessary defining historical term

Page 13

1 A = f; B = e; C = a; D = d; E = b; F = c

2
  a A, B, C
  b A, C, D
  c A, B, C

3 B

Page 14

4 A = b; B = d; C = c; D = a

5
  a Abbots – they oversee monasteries, the others hold senior positions in churches.
  b York – it is an archbishopric, the others are bishoprics.
  c Sheriff – all of the others were roles undertaken by clergy for the king.

6
  A True
  B True
  C False
  D False
  E True
  F False
  G False
  H False

Page 15

1 A, B, D, E, F

2 In Norman England, the Church was a major landholder. It got its land from the king, like everyone else in ~~William's new social hierarchy, with him firmly at the top~~. (A) Bishops, like earls, were ~~immediately under the king and got their land directly from him~~(E) so had to provide him with ~~knights for forty days each year at their own expense.~~(C) They were also required to ~~publicly demonstrate their allegiance to William in a special ceremony~~(B) in return for their fiefs. This made the Church subordinate to the king and useful for controlling England. Lanfranc especially was very loyal to William, even though the pope expected clergy to obey him first rather than ~~non ecclesiastical or non religious~~, (D) leaders.

Page 16

1 B

2 The opening sentence of a paragraph should make the point that the paragraph is to be about. Statement C focuses on Norman government rather than the Church, and would lead to a paragraph that doesn't fit the question properly.

3 unnecessary description: a, c

not focused on the question: a, d

4 Answers might vary but B → b, e, f, g.

Page 17

1 <mark>One reason for Lanfranc's reforms</mark> was to strengthen Norman control over England. One reform was to rebuild Church buildings. This was important for two reasons. Firstly, they would be made to look Norman, using Norman architectural features such as high, vaulted ceilings. They would be a visual reminder to the Anglo-Saxons of God favouring William at Hastings. Secondly, and more importantly, cathedrals in isolated locations (like Thetford) were demolished and rebuilt in strategically important market towns (like Norwich). <u>This made Norman bishops more secure and enabled them to better control their clergy and their flocks. Thus this important reform was aimed at strengthening William's grip on England</u> and the Anglo-Saxons.

There is no filler material.

Page 18

1

Strengths		Weaknesses	
Paragraph opens with a clear point about why Lanfranc reformed the Church in England.	1 & 2	Paragraph contains unnecessary or irrelevant information (filler).	1 & 2
Paragraph ends with a clear link back to the question.	2	Paragraph wanders off the question focus.	1
A reason for Lanfranc's reforms is clearly explained with relevant evidence.	1 & 2	Paragraph contains unnecessary explanation of historical terms.	1 & 2

2 Student's own response, but likely to be 4/6: More focused than not.

Page 9

1 Student's own response.

Unit 3

Page 22

1

How well does each plan …	Very well	Quite well	Not at all
show a wide variety of reasons?	A	B	
show how one cause leads to another and so on?	B		A
show how causes interact with each other?		B	A

Page 23

1 B, C
2 B, C, D
3 D
4 A, B, C, D
5 A = 5 (1065)
B = 6 (1066)
C = 2 (1053)
D = 3 (1055)
E = 4 (1062)
F = 1 (1045)
6 A = d
B = c
C = a
D = b
E = e
F = a

2 and **3** Student's own response, but the answer should look like:

<mark>Improve Church discipline = reform aim.</mark> <mark>Unify the English Church under Norman guidelines and standards; strict hierarchy, but under William – not the pope.</mark> Also, William = head of feudal system;

bishops held land as vassals. <mark>Reforms for discipline = (i) unify Church; (ii) more archdeacons to enforce Church discipline, e.g. preside over Church courts; (iii) Church courts = reform to control parish priests.</mark>

Page 24

7 a Siward – all the others were Earl Godwin's children.
b Harold Godwinson – all the others have a connection to Northumbria.
c Forging silver pennies – all the others were crimes committed by Tostig as Earl of Northumbria.
d Making laws – all the others were duties of the earls.

8 By persuading Edward to appoint bishops loyal to them.

9 Judith of Flanders

10 a Tostig replaced Siward as Earl of Northumbria **or** Morcar replaced Tostig as Earl of Northumbria.
b Edward's order to send an army against Tostig was ignored.
c By the 1060s the Godwins controlled most of England.
d The Vikings remained a threat to England under Edward the Confessor.
e In 1062 Harold and Tostig attacked Llewelyn.
f In 1062 Harold Godwinson led a fleet against the Welsh.

Page 25

1 a and b Student's own response, but it needs to be a logical sequence. Examples could include:

G could be caused by J and could lead to C, E, H, L.

B could be caused by L and could lead to D, J.

Note: If F is chosen, column 1 will be blank.

2 A → J → B → D
K → J → C & E → H → I

Page 26

1 A Members of the House of Godwin were given earldoms across England and (consequently) became militarily strong. There was a family tie (because) Edward married Edith. Wessex was important for England's defence. This (caused) Edward to rely on Harold Godwinson. B Secondly, the threat from Wales (led to) the House of

Godwin becoming stronger still. Tostig and Harold joined together to defeat Llewelyn in 1062. This (resulted in) the Welsh being much less of a threat to Edward, but it (led Harold to) assume the role of sub-regulus and (in turn) appoint his own puppet king to lead Wales. The (consequence of) this was that Edward had been sidelined by Harold.

②

Strengths	A, B or both?	Weaknesses	A, B or both?
Clear focus to the paragraph	B	Paragraph focus uncertain	A
Causation is explained	B	A series of statements about cause	A
Specific supporting evidence	B	Undeveloped historical knowledge	A

③ Student's own responses, but a possible solution is as follows.

Edward was a weak king <u>because</u> his religious, peaceable nature was not suited to medieval kingship, which <u>led him</u> to rely on the big earldoms' military forces. <u>Consequently</u>, the likes of Harold and Tostig developed their own powerbases in Wessex and Northumbria, <u>resulting in</u> them being more powerful than Edward. The Godwinson victory over Llewelyn in 1062 is a fine example. It <u>led</u> Harold to appoint a new Welsh king who was his puppet, <u>in turn</u> making Harold Edward's effective sub-regulus and <u>consequently</u> undermining Edward.

Page 27

① Student's own response, but, based on the evidence provided, C clearly had an impact. G, D and H were also key in the House of Godwin becoming more powerful than Edward the Confessor.

② Student's own response, although C is likely to be seen as a root cause.

③ B is the best choice as it gives key points in the causal chain whereas A goes through the whole causal process again.

Page 28

① A is the better plan because it:
- clearly shows causation
- combines causation with evidence to develop a causal argument
- has strong links back to the question
- highlights other important causes.

B has a lot of information, but also paragraphs that simply string a lot of causes together.

Page 29

① Student's own response.

Unit 4

Page 32

① A = a, b, d
B = a, c, e, g
C = a, b, d
D = b, d
E = a, e, f

② Student's own response, but ought to include some from each of the following:
A = a, b, c, f, h
B = e, f, g
C = a, b, c, d, f, h
D = a, b, h
E = a, b, c, d, f, h
F = a, b, c, f,
G = e, g
H = a, b, c, e, f, h

Page 33

① 1066: F
1067: G
1068: E
1069 (February): C
1069 (September): B
1069–70: H
1070–71: A
1075: D

②
a Odo
b Morcar
c Durham
d waste
e five
f King Sweyn
g FitzOsbern
h geld
i Ely
j Hereford
k Wessex
l Edgar

O	D	F	I	V	E	F	Q	I	E
H	D	M	V	E	W	I	K	H	D
E	F	O	R	T	N	T	I	C	G
R	O	R	A	S	B	Z	N	O	A
E	L	C	W	A	B	O	G	I	R
F	E	A	E	W	E	S	S	E	X
O	F	R	E	L	U	B	W	A	E
R	O	G	R	L	Y	E	E	D	A
D	U	R	H	A	M	R	Y	W	R
X	G	E	L	D	F	N	N	A	I

Page 34

③
a William secured the south of England by destroying it and/or by force.
b William declared that, because he was king, all England belonged to him.

c. Building castles was William's way of dominating (or controlling) the Anglo-Saxons/providing strategic bases for his lords.
d. Under William, sheriffs were answerable to the king.
e. The Danes left England in autumn 1069 because William paid them to.
f. The 1069 rebellions occurred in the north-east of England, along the Welsh Marches (or in Shropshire in the west, and Staffordshire in the north midlands) and in Devon.

4. A, B, D
5. D
6. B, C
7. A, B
8. a. False
   b. True

Page 35

1.

Political context 1066	1068	Post-1071
There were both Norman and Anglo-Saxon earls	No change	Far fewer Anglo-Saxons – Waltheof Earl of Northumbria; Mercia, East Anglia under Norman control
Anglo-Saxon earls submitted to William	Several earls rebelled	Waltheof was the only Anglo-Saxon earl who rebelled after 1071
William brought southern England firmly under his control	No change	No change
Fortified burhs protected the people	Changing: Norman castles being built	Many more castles built, especially if there were rebellions (e.g. Warwick)
Religious context 1066	**1069**	**Post-1071**
Anglo-Saxon clergy remained in place	No change	Normanisation of the Church
The Danish threat 1066	**1069**	**Post-1071**
William's concern about Danish intervention in, and raids on, England	No change	No change – William remained concerned about Danish invasion throughout his reign
Northern England harder to govern, heavily influenced by Danelaw	No change	After Harrying of the North, Danelaw and northern England were severely weakened

2. William had changed his tactics and had begun to treat Anglo-Saxon landholders more aggressively, resulting in their loss of land and power. As a result, they had fewer resources with which to rebel.

Page 36

1. He gets angrier and harsher.

2.

Date	Change in context
1069–70	Harrying of the North weakened northern England, which had been the focus of most rebellion; laid waste to Yorkshire
1070	Purge and Normanisation of English Church → Norman control
1071	William's approach to landholding changes; Mercia, East Anglia, other Anglo-Saxon lands in north → given to Norman earls; consolidates earldoms, smaller → easier to control; thegns have to obey new Norman lords or leave England

3. Student's own response, but ought to mention, for example, William's changes in landholding and possibly Normanisation of the Church as part of this.

Page 37

1.

Domestic context	1066	Post-1071
William wanted to appear to be upholding Anglo-Saxon laws and traditions	✓	
Norman castles had been built across England		✓
Northern England, Mercia and East Anglia were governed by Norman earls		✓
The feudal system had been established		✓
Context of Danish threat		
Northern England was heavily influenced by Danelaw, strong links with Danes	✓	
William was concerned about Danish raids/invasions	✓	✓

2. a. Responses will vary, although they are likely to be 1 or 2 as the changing context gave William a much stronger grip on England, especially the North.
   b. Student's own response.

3. Responses will vary, but are likely to be 'largely context' or 'more context than Danes'.

4. Student's own response.

Page 38

1. a – d

If the Danes' support had been so important to Anglo-Saxon resistance, then there would not have been attacks by Eadric and the Welsh in 1067, nor the rebellion in 1068, as the Danes took part in neither. The Danes did support Edgar in 1069 and Hereward in 1070–71. It is also true that 1071 marked the end of Anglo-Saxon resistance and the end of Danish support coincided with it because it was not needed any more.

In 1069–70, the Harrying of the North was a turning point in the political context* of England. Instead of winning over the Anglo-Saxon aristocracy, William began replacing them. The Harrying of the North was William's revenge for Anglo-Saxon resistance there; as many as 100,000 people died. In 1071 Edwin and Morcar joined Hereward, forfeiting their lands in Northumbria, Mercia and East Anglia to men loyal to William. William also reduced the size of earldoms and consolidated them, so it was harder for Anglo-Saxons to resist. In 1070 the Church was Normanised, and its posts and lands transferred to Normans. By 1075, political circumstances had changed so Normans had complete control of England*. The 1075 revolt was basically Norman-led, as William's changes upset the Norman earls of Hereford and East Anglia. The only Anglo-Saxon earl involved in 1075 was Waltheof of Northumbria; he was executed at Winchester in 1076.

- e Student's own response.

Page 39

1. Student's own response.

Unit 5

Page 42

1.

Evidence of economic gain as a reason	Evidence of defence as a reason	Evidence of political power as a reason
A, C, D	E, I, J	B, C, F, G, H, I

2.
   - a Column 3 – political power
   - b Student's own response, but likely to be 'largely', given the evidence.
3. Evidence C
4. Evidence C links strongly with: B, F, H. It also links to I, J.
5. Student's own response. Likely to be 'very little', as the evidence linking to c shows that changing landholding patterns was more about power than revenue, **although the two are quite closely linked.**

Page 43

1. A = e; B = a; C = d; D = f; E = c; F = b
2.
   - a True
   - b True
   - c False
   - d False
   - e False
   - f False
3. A = 3, B = 5, C = 4, D = 1, E = 2, F = 6

Page 44

4.
   - a By 1087 there were only **two** Anglo-Saxon tenants-in-chief.
   - b Norman **sheriffs** were notorious for corruptly seizing land.
   - c If Anglo-Saxon landholders wanted to keep using their own land they had to pay **to redeem it**.
   - d The land of landholders who died without heirs was given to the **king**.
   - e After 1071 William made sure his landholders' land was **consolidated into blocks**.
   - f Under the feudal system thegns could be dispossessed by **their tenant-in-chief**.

5.
   - a C
   - b A, B, D
   - c B
   - d A
   - e B, C, D

Page 45

1.

Reason	Strong government	Defence	Revenues	Crush Anglo-Saxon resistance
Evidence	C, F, H, I	A, C, D	A, B, C, E, G	A, C, F, I

2. Revenues
3. There is room for discussion with this. All three measures helped William considerably. The most likely response for D and F is 'maybe'. Regarding I, the answer should be either 'maybe' or 'no way.' It is **possible** that William could have remained king, but it would have been extremely difficult as thegns were often very rebellious. The threat of being dispossessed was an important means of control.

	Yes, probably	Maybe	No way
D		✓	
F		✓	
I		✓	✓

4. Student's own response, though it should be reasoned effectively. The answer ought to be c, as it underpinned the feudal system, control of land and revenues.
5.
   - a Yes (based on the answer to 4 being c).
   - b Significance of evidence is more effective. One piece of evidence can have a greater impact than several smaller ones.

Page 46

1.

Situation after 1070	Before 1070?
William focused more on practical solutions for maintaining control	✓*
Harrying of the North → William replaces Anglo-Saxon aristocracy there	
Normanisation of the Church: all but one bishop was Norman	
William, Odo, FitzOsbern held land in the strategic south and, south-east	✓
Marcher earls had the same powers and obligations as other earls	
Size of earldoms generally reduced, including Norman earldoms	

*It could be said that this was William's main goal from the outset (although this does say *more* focused). However, the Harrying of the North and the 1071 rebellions mark a change in William's approach. William became less concerned about presenting himself as keeping to Anglo-Saxon law and traditions and more concerned about to wanting to replace

Anglo-Saxon earls and crack down on rebellion. The change in his attitude towards Edwin and Morcar in 1071 compared with 1068 shows this clearly.

(2) a William was keen to present himself as keeping to Anglo-Saxon law and traditions because he thought it would be an effective way of strengthening his position/it might win over the Anglo-Saxons.

b William focused more on practical solutions because he needed to control/reduce the number of Anglo-Saxon earldoms after much unrest/several rebellions between 1066 and 1071.

(3) Student's own response, but it ought to mention the change in William's approach after 1070–71.

Page 47

(1) The crushing of Anglo-Saxon resistance.

(2) a Student's own response, but some examples are

Aim A had a knock-on effect on C and D.

Aim B had a knock-on effect on C, D (the more revenues, the easier C and D were).

Aim C had a knock-on effect on A and D. (A as William needed to give border lands to loyal followers and at first the Marcher earls also had more power and wealth than others. D because England's borders were often places where rebellions began, e.g. 1069 or Hereward the Wake).

Aim D had a knock-on effect on A, B and C. (A because earls who forfeited their land enabled William to either take their land and keep it, or pass it on to loyal subjects. B because of the cost involved in crushing Anglo-Saxon resistance – the Harrying of the North had a very negative impact on Crown revenues; also by increasing the amount of land held directly by William. C because the Harrying of the North and its impact on Danelaw ended Viking activity in the North.)

b Student's own response, but likely to be D – crushing Anglo-Saxon resistance.

Page 48

(1)

Has the answer ...	A	B	C
clearly highlighted the most significant cause?			✓
supported it with specific evidence?	✓	✓	✓
shown how it impacted on other factors?		✓	✓
shown any change of significant factor over time?		✓	✓

Page 49

(1) and (2) Student's own response.

Unit 6

Page 52

(1) a & b

Intro:
~~Overview of the circumstances leading William to undertake the Harrying of the North.~~

Paragraph 1
~~Harrying of the North: after serious 1069 rebellion when Edgar had Danish support, plus rebellion often focused on north; also northern rebellion often → rebellions elsewhere in England. Rebels didn't fight in open battle so William used same tactics as in south in 1066.~~

Paragraph 2
Up to 100,000 people died – killed, starved, frozen to death: homes burned, crops destroyed, reports of cannibalism; people going into slavery for food; refugee crisis – thousands fled.

Paragraph 3
~~William realised north of England different from south and harder to govern too – Danelaw. Explain Danelaw, link to Vikings. England always under threat from Viking invasions.~~

~~Harrying of the North weakened Danelaw: Hereward/Viking rebellion 1070–71 in East Anglia.~~

Paragraph 4
Pope and Church angry about Harrying of the North. William regretted it → money and time to Church; plus made Anglo-Saxon Waltheof Earl of Northumbria 1072 – gesture of reconciliation?

Conclusion
William regretted Harrying of the North for the rest of his life (remorse – gave money to Church; financial losses too), so more than just destruction of crops.

(2) Partially – 2/4 paragraphs

Page 53

(1) a Edwin and Morcar's rebellion: 1068
b Harrying of the North: 1069–70
c Hereward the Wake's rebellion: 1070–71
d The Battle of Hastings: 1066
e Edgar Aethling and the Vikings attack York: 1069

(2) A = d; B = c; C = a; D = f; E = e; F = b

(3) D

(4) A, B, D

(5) B

(6) B, C

Page 54

(7) a True
b False
c False
d False
e False
f False

(8) a Sixty per cent of Yorkshire was still classed as waste when the Domesday Book was compiled.

b Hereward the Wake was the last example of Anglo-Saxon resistance. ('The Harrying of the North was **not** the last example of Anglo-Saxon resistance' does not count.)

c There may have been 80,000 fewer oxen and 150,000 fewer people in Yorkshire in 1086 than there were in 1066.

d Either: William wanted to meet the rebels in the North in open battle **or** The rebels in the North would not meet William in open battle.

  e The area laid waste by William stretched from the River Humber to the River Tees.

9 a Herefordshire – the other three were laid waste, wholly or in part, by William.

  b Excommunication – the others were all problems that resulted from the Harrying of the North.

  c 1067 – there were significant rebellions in all of the other years.

Page 55

1 a A, C, G, J

  b B, D, E, F, H, I

2 a and b

The Harrying of the North led to Yorkshire being laid to waste, disrupting farming, which in turn led to starvation and refugees fleeing the region. It had the desired effect of putting a stop to rebellion in the North. This had been one of William's aims. Rebellion in the North often led to rebellions elsewhere. It was also a problem as the Danelaw led to close links with Vikings. As well as the deaths of up to 100,000 people, the Harrying destroyed farmland and related economic activities as long afterwards as 1086, resulting in falling revenues from the North.

  c B, F (homelessness), H, I.

Page 56

1 Cross out B, C, D and E

2 Harrying of the North → H → G → F → William secure on throne until his death

3

Consequence	Immediate (short term)	Long term	Intended	Unintended
William regretted the Harrying for the rest of his life		✓		✓
Thousands starved and froze to death*	✓		✓	
End to rebellion focused on the North		✓	✓	

*Arguable, but what else would the destruction of crops, livestock, next year's seeds and people's homes lead to?

Page 57

1 Student's own response. Possibly E → B → C → D, though there are other solutions.

2 Student's own response. There must be a convincing reason. This would depend upon whose point of view: the question asks for a Norman point of view but you might like to consider how different an Anglo-Saxon point of view would be.

3

Consequence	1066	1069–70
Positive	A, B, C	A, C
Negative		B
Short term		B*
Long term	A, B, C	A, B, C

*This depends on whether you are looking at only William's reign **or** Norman England.

Page 58

1 a–d

The Harrying of the North had very important consequences for William. It is said that he regretted it for the rest of his life. It resulted in there being no more rebellions in the north of England. This was possibly the most significant consequence for William, as rebellions there triggered them elsewhere, stretching his resources. So for him it was a very positive outcome and to this extent he achieved his aim. However, there was the unintended and very negative consequence of the pope's criticism and William spending a lot of time and money making amends.

Perhaps the most shocking consequence was the deaths of up to 100,000 people. Some historians say it was a genocide.

The Harrying led to the immediate consequence of the destruction of farming*, with the knock-on effect of thousands starving to death in the next year or so. As farming was the main economic activity and source of income, its devastation had knock-on, long-term impacts on almost all parts of the North's economy too. In 1086, the Domesday Book recorded that 60 per cent of Yorkshire was still waste. This would not have been what William intended, as his revenues suffered in the long run as a consequence. It was certainly a negative consequence for him and far worse for the people of the North.

Page 59

1 and **2** Student's own response.

Unit 7

Page 62

1 a One (statement 2 only).

  b C – Not very important

  c A: statements 4, 6 and 8 directly; plus 7; quite important

   B: statements 1, 2, 3, 5 and 7; very important

   C: statements 1, 3; not very important

2 First, the weakness of the earls' position; second, the earls' self-interest; third, Edgar Aethling was not a credible alternative; lastly, fear of William.

3 Student's own response. Answers will probably focus on the significance of the evidence – for example, William's laying waste to south-east England must have had a huge impact on the earls, although the quantity of evidence suggests it was not very important.

Page 63

1. A, B, D
2. B, C, D
3. B, C, D
4. A, C, D
5.
   a. False
   b. False
   c. True
   d. False
   e. False
   f. True

Page 64

6. C
7. A
8. D
9. C
10.
    a. Winchester was where England's Treasury was.
    b. 25 December 1066
    c. The right to their land.
11.
    a. After Hastings, William allowed Edwin and FitzOsbern to keep much of their land.
    b. William met with Archbishop Stigand at Wallingford to negotiate the terms of the submission of the earls.
    c. William's brutal strategy in the south of England led to towns on his way to London surrendering.
    d. Gospatric was made Earl of northern Northumbria after paying William a large sum of money.

Page 65

1.

Evidence suggesting fear of William was important	Evidence linking fear of William to other causes	Evidence suggesting fear of William was not important
William had brutally destroyed swathes of the south-east after the Battle of Hastings	Student's own response but could include evidence showing the earls' position was weak: William had secured the south and supply routes to Normandy; although the earls held London, William's route threatened to cut it off from reinforcements from the North. Possibly could include evidence that Edgar Aethling was not credible as a leader to oppose William.	Student's own response but likely to include: Edgar Aethling was not credible: he had been considered too young to be king after Edward died; he had only recently arrived in England, without any 'ready-made' support. Earls' self-interest: The earls submitted in return for William promising to be a 'good and gracious lord'; William showed no signs of wanting to replace all Anglo-Saxons in high positions, e.g. Anglo-Saxon bishops and archbishops were to keep their positions; William promised that Edwin could marry his daughter, which could have made him very powerful in the new, Norman kingdom.

2. Student's own response, but likely to be at least agree more than disagree, depending on how much importance is attached to evidence that links to fear (column 2).
3. Plan B because it has a tight question focus. The stated factor is dealt with from the outset and in each paragraph its importance compared with other factors is explained; there is a clear judgement as to what is the most important reason and why.

Page 66

1.
   a. According to B, the Anglo-Saxon earls had shown they were willing to carry on by electing Edgar as king. It was only once they were all in London, as described in A, that they realised that continuing was not possible.
   b. C and D see the earls' actions differently. C is positive, seeing the nobles as wanting to fight on but being swayed by the loss of the Treasury. D, however, is negative, seeing the nobles as self-serving when William made them offers they couldn't refuse.

2.
   a. Student's own response, but an example is: Although Edgar's lack of credibility was important, the weakness of the earls' position was perhaps more important. While Edgar being a poor choice of king contributed to the earls' weakness, it would not on its own have prevented a fight back; lack of resources did.
   b. Student's own response. Although the earls' self-interest was certainly a factor in their submission, fear of William can be seen as more important because the consequences of fighting on would have hurt their self-interest even more. Submitting to William in return for him being a 'good and gracious lord' was a very significant factor, but it can be argued that fear for their lives was the most important reason why the earls submitted.

Page 67

1. Self-interest → submission of the earls: Edwin to marry William's daughter; earls kept much of their land: Mercia (Edwin), Northumbria (Morcar); Anglo-Saxons continued to hold all top Church positions; William promising to be a 'good and gracious' lord to the Anglo-Saxons.

Earls' position weak: William held the south coast of England; his brutal progress → southern towns quickly surrendering; earls in London: William in danger of cutting them off from supplies and reinforcements from the north; Edgar not effective, couldn't agree with earls on what to do.

2 Student's own response. The table below identifies evidence for and against. Answers will vary, but likely to be less fear of William than other reasons.

Evidence yes, it was fear of William	Evidence no, it wasn't
Battle of Hastings = crushing defeat, many of the best warriors in England had been killed.	There was no immediate surrender after the Battle of Hastings, despite William's reputation and actions before the battle. Instead, the Witan elected Edgar king. However, Edgar had only recently arrived in England, without ready-made support. He took no decisive action as king, probably because he and the earls couldn't agree on what to do.
Destroying everything in his path was a brutally effective strategy. People rushed to submit rather than face destruction. William intimidated Anglo-Saxons, including those in towns on the way to, and around, London. William led his troops west, continuing their path of destruction, until they reached Berkhamsted.	William took Winchester and the Treasury. Without the treasury in Winchester (held by William), Edgar could not reward followers, while William could.
	William had control of Wessex and the south coast.
	The earls went to London, which was strongly fortified. William would lose a lot of men if he attacked it directly. This suggests they intended to fight on.
	Even before Hastings, William allowed his men to cause great destruction in the surrounding area: they laid waste to their surroundings too, burning down houses.	The earls submitted in return for William's promise to be good and gracious: earls like Edwin and Morcar kept their earldoms, archbishops like Stigand and Ealdred kept their positions. William promised that Edwin could marry his daughter, which would have made Edwin very powerful in the new kingdom if it had happened.

Page 68

1 a–e

Fear of William was an important factor in the submission of the earls in 1066. By the time he had reached Berkhamsted, William had destroyed south-east England. From one point of view fear of William can be seen as important because of its impact on southern England; from another it was the earls' self-interest that was.* Events in southern England suggested that the earls were likely to lose and could expect harsh treatment from William.

More important, however, was the weakness of the earls' position. Fear of William led towns to surrender to him and reinforced this weakness*, especially as he had taken Winchester, and so the Treasury. This meant that there was no way to pay for another army even if one could be raised. Edgar, although elected king by the Witan, had only recently returned to England and had no army of his own. He took no decisive action against William, suggesting either a lack of experience or that he and the earls could not agree about what to do. Although it is true that the weakness of the earls' position was most important to their submission, it is also true that Edgar's lack of credibility was at least partly a reason for that.* Likewise, while the earls' own self-interest was partly a factor, the weakness of their position was more important because* by the time they submitted it was so bad that there was little real alternative.

Page 69

1 **a** Student's own response, but table should look something like this.

Evidence yes, it was self-interest	Evidence no, it wasn't
The earls submitted in return for William's promise to be good and gracious: earls like Edwin and Morcar kept their earldoms, archbishops like Stigand and Ealdred kept their positions. William promised that Edwin could marry his daughter, which would have made Edwin very powerful in the new kingdom if it had happened.	There was no immediate surrender after the Battle of Hastings, despite William's reputation and actions before the battle. Instead, the Witan elected Edgar king. However, Edgar had only recently arrived in England, without ready-made support. He took no decisive action as king, probably because he and the earls couldn't agree on what to do.
	William took Winchester and the Treasury. Without the treasury in Winchester (held by William), Edgar could not reward followers, while William could.
	William had control of Wessex and the south coast.
	The earls went to London, which was strongly fortified. William would lose a lot of men if he attacked it directly. This suggests they intended to fight on.
	Battle of Hastings = crushing defeat, many of the best warriors in England had been killed.
Note: Self-interest can also include staying alive. In this sense, the weakness of the earls' position compared with William's and fear of William could also be linked. This is the student's own decision.	Destroying everything in his path was a brutally effective strategy. People rushed to submit rather than face destruction. William intimidated Anglo-Saxons, including towns on the way to, and around, London. William led his troops west, continuing their path of destruction, until they reached Berkhamsted.
	Even before Hastings, William allowed his men to cause great destruction in the surrounding area: they laid waste to their surroundings too, burning down houses.

2–**5** Student's own response.

Unit 8

Page 72

1 **a** Amy's choice of evidence focuses more on the feudal system. Amy wrote conclusion 3.

  b Sanjay's evidence focuses more on the role of sheriffs. Sanjay wrote conclusion 1.

2 Amy:

The feudal system enabled William's centralisation of power. Since he was king, even the tenants-in-chief were answerable to him, and he used grants and forfeits of land to keep them loyal (**E**). Even their knights owed direct loyalty to the king (**D**). Furthermore, thegns were replaced by knights (**C**). These changes gave William more control than increasing royal demesne (**A**).

Sanjay:

The most important reason that William could centralise power was the sheriffs. They enforced his new laws against rebellion (**F**), were the undisputed leaders of their shires and answered only to William (**B**). This gave William control over more land than just the royal demesne. It also reduced the power of tenants-in-chief, whose knights owed their loyalty directly to the king (**D**).

3 Conclusion 1 because it considers a wider range of reasons to explain how the judgement was reached.

Page 73

1 A = d; B = f; C = b; D = e; E = c; F = a; G = h; H = g.

2 William introduced payments called **reliefs** that landholders' **heirs** made to reclaim their inheritance. The amount was decided by **William**, and he rewarded **loyalty** by agreeing small amounts. He could also use **forfeits** of land to punish disobedient **vassals**. During his reign, William decreased the size of **earldoms** and increased the **royal demesne**. Fines for breaking the harsh **forest** laws were a very good source of **income** for William.

3 A What William's tenants-in-chief (and their tenants) were worth/a detailed survey of landholding/who owned what land and so owed taxes or obligations.

Page 74

4 **a** Homage – the others are all forms of revenue

  b Slaves – the others all have a place in the feudal system

  c Knights – the others were all appointed by William

  d Regent – all the others are types of court

5 B and C

6 A, B, C, D

7 B and D

8 A, B and C

9 **a** Those who killed deer in the royal forest were blinded.

  b Student's own response, such as: there was no such thing as the geld tax in Normandy/William kept the Anglo-Saxon geld tax.

  c Sheriffs were often castellans/castellans were often sheriffs.

  d New bishops paid homage to the king.

Page 75

1 **a–d** Answers may vary slightly.

Although increasing the royal demesne was quite significant in William centralising power because he increased his own landholding, revenues and therefore power, the feudal system and sheriffs were more important. Sheriffs, as the undisputed leaders of the shires answerable only to the king, helped William to strengthen his grip on power more directly. The feudal system was most important because as its head, William used grants and forfeits to directly control potentially powerful earls. Powerful earls could undermine the king. Overall, the feudal system was much more important than increasing the royal demesne in William centralising power, because it was the feudal system that gave him control over those most likely to be a challenge to him.

2 **a** Statement B

  b Statement A: Increasing the royal demesne was simply another way of reducing the size of the earldoms and so was less important to centralising power.

  Statement B: Reducing the size of earldoms was much more important to William centralising power than increasing the royal demesne.

  Statement C: Reducing the size of the earldoms was more important because it enabled William to control the earls better, and the earls to control their lands more effectively.

Page 76

1 **a** D, G

  b B, E, F

  c A, C, D, F, H

2 Student's own response, but the evidence points most clearly to C (the feudal system).

3 Student's own response, but A is probably the best as it underpins much of the other evidence provided. The key is that the reason given is clear and logical.

4 Student's own response.

Page 77

1

Key characteristics of a strong conclusion		Which statement shows which characteristic?
a	Statement giving what you believe to be the most important factor	D
b	Statement on how far you agree with the stated factor	A
c	Explanation of your choice of most important element and why it is more important than any others	B & F
d	Bring in the relative importance of any other factors	E

e	Reinforce your conclusion about the most important factor and how it relates to the stated and other factors	E
f	Statement giving what you believe to be the most important factor	D

Page 78

1. The feudal system.

2. The feudal system that William imposed ensured that tenants-in-chief and their knights <u>owed loyalty to him</u> and this kept them within his control. <u>Land could be granted but also forfeited, so William could directly control the fates of earls</u>. Although earls could be sheriffs, William could also take the position away from them if he wished. William's powerful position at the top of <u>the feudal system was reinforced by the Normanisation of the Church</u>. <u>Not only were bishops also tenants-in-chief</u> (so they were part of the feudal system), but <u>they also ensured that the people accepted William's government</u> because he had God's approval, as Hastings had shown. The sheriffs were undisputed leaders of the shires, answerable only to the king.

3. Normanisation of the Church.

4. Because the Church and clergy were part of the feudal system, so the Normanisation of the Church simply reinforced it.

5. Student's own response, but it ought to use the wording of the question to highlight the judgement that the essay has made/led to. It should deal with the 'how far' part of the question too.

6. Student's own response, but it ought to finally emphasise the judgement given in direct answer to the question.

Page 79

1. Students' own response, but it ought to follow the checklist.